A TIME TO BE BORN

Bonnie Shullenberger

COWLEY PUBLICATIONS

Cambridge ✦ *Boston*
Massachusetts

Published in the United States of America by Cowley Publications, a division of the Society of St. John the Evangelist. No portion of this book may be reproduced, stored in or introduced into a retrieval system, or transmitted, in any form or by any means— including photocopying—without the prior written permission of Cowley Publications, except in the case of brief quotations embodied in critical articles and reviews.

Library of Congress Cataloging-in-Publication Data:
Shullenberger, Bonnie, 1948-
  A time to be born / Bonnie Shullenberger.
     p.   cm.
  Includes bibliographical references.
  ISBN: 1-56101-131-2 (alk. paper)
    1. Shullenberger, Bonnie, 1948- . 2. Abortion—Moral and ethical aspects. 3. Abortion—Religious aspects—Episcopal Church. 4. Pregnancy, Unwanted—United States—Case studies. 5. Adoption—United States—Case studies. 6. Episcopalians—United States—Biography. I. Title.
HQ767.15.S53 1996
363.4'6'092—dc20   96-24911
                                          CIP

The material on pages 61-67 appeared in an earlier version in *The Living Church*, July 23, 1989. The material on pages 99-102 previously appeared in *Sharing: A Journal of Christian Healing*, in May, 1991. The author is grateful to both journals for permission to reprint these passages.

Scripture quotations are from the *New Revised Standard Version* of the Bible, © 1989 by the Division of Christian Education of the National Council of the Churches of Christ in the USA. Used by permission. All rights reserved.

Editor: Cynthia Shattuck.
Copyeditor and Designer: Vicki Black.
Cover Design: Vicki Black.

With the exception of the names of the author's husband and children, and scholars whose work is publicly known, names in this narrative have been changed.

This book is printed on acid-free paper and was produced in the United States of America.

Cowley Publications
28 Temple Place
Boston, Massachusetts 02111

A Time to Be Born

Dedicated to Shannon, Geoff, and David

I will give thanks to the Lord with my whole heart,
in the company of the upright, in the congregation.
Great are the works of the Lord,
studied by all who delight in them.
(Psalm 111:1-2)

CONTENTS

IN
GRATITUDE

There are many people to whom I am grateful for their assistance and love as I worked on this book:

Cynthia Shattuck of Cowley Publications,
wise midwife to the manuscript;

Victor Austin, Elaine Counsell, Bill Doubleday, Anne English,
Peter Hawkins, Marjorie Kivell, and Frederica Mathewes-Green;

Many Ugandans, especially Mabel Katahweire, Susan Kiguli,
Grace Ndyabahika, and Hellen Wangusa, and my students;

Geoff, for being patient when I was hogging the computer;

My dad, for teaching me to tell stories, and my mom, for show-
ing me what it means to hang on no matter how badly it hurts;

And Bill, lover, brother in Christ, brave companion of the road,
for all the reasons in the world.

FOREWORD

by Stanley Hauerwas

This is a book about abortion. This is not a book about abortion. Both of these statements are true and false and how they are true and false says everything about this book. The book is about abortion—or better, it is about the abortion Bonnie Shullenberger did not have. Yet it is also a story of the life Bonnie Shullenberger has led that makes her decision not to have an abortion intelligible.

It is accordingly a wonderful book. I cried often as I read her story. Tears are appropriate for a story told so honestly and in such an unguarded fashion. That Bonnie Shullenberger can tell her story so straightforwardly has everything to do with her being a Christian, for all God has left her with is her honesty. It is now a gift she gives to us in the hope that her story may help us all live more decent and faithful lives.

Stories like Bonnie's are what we must have if we are to think clearly as well as live responsibly with one another when facing matters such as abortion. Such stories provide witnesses that make arguments about abortion serious. So often the arguments on both sides sound empty and unconvincing exactly because the arguments are quite literally lifeless. Here we have a life that our arguments must exemplify if they are to help us care for and support one another.

Bonnie Shullenberger, moreover, is a mature and sophisticated witness. She is, after all, "liberated." A child of the sixties, pregnant out of wedlock, married and divorced, married with two children, she is not exactly "innocent." Thank God she is not. Innocence could never write with such insight and power that helps her remember the pain that would tempt her to forget what it means to give up a child. Accordingly, her life becomes a witness just to the extent she can remember. As she says, "Thank God for memory," because without memory we would be condemned to repeat our sin just to the extent we feel it necessary to justify ourselves.

Such memory is possible, as Shullenberger makes clear, because as Christians we live by forgiveness. Not forgiveness we give, but forgiveness we receive. Such forgiveness makes it possible for us to remember that indeed we might be tempted and may possibly even have an abortion but by God's grace we do not have to call it good. More important, she challenges Christians to be the kind of people who can make lives like her own possible and can save us from the assumption that abortion is an alternative for us. Instead, she calls us to be the kind of community that can receive women and children into our lives in a manner that abortion just does not have to come up.

This is the story of how Bonnie Shullenberger became a Christian. It is the story of how she became a priest. It is, more importantly, a story about God's continuing power in her life and in our lives. It was God who spoke through Hannah, her Jewish communist friend who said that abortion is murder. It was God who led her through her odd fascination with Christianity to become a Christian who knows that God speaks through Hannah and another Jewish girl named Mary. God surrounds our lives with witnesses named Hannah, Mary, Bonnie so that we might be protected from those who would have us kill in the name of freedom.

Such people constitute an army, an army of salvation like the one that saw Shullenberger through her first pregnancy, by which the world may know there is an alternative to abortion. The harsh tenderness she found in the nurses and the cooks at the Catherine Booth Residence for unwed mothers pervades her story as she tries to help us all discover a better way.

The arguments will continue about abortion, convincing no one. Witnesses like Bonnie Shullenberger make the difference. Thank God she has given us her story.

ONE

It is January 1967. The top hits on the radio are the Mamas and the Papas with their least interesting song, "Words of Love," Paul Revere and the Raiders with "Good Thing," and Nancy Sinatra's "Sugartown." Paul Revere and the Raiders no longer dress up in Revolutionary War costumes, nor do they sing moralistic, anti-counterculture songs like "Kicks," and whether Nancy Sinatra knows that the hippies think her song is about sugar cubes laced with LSD is not at all clear. In any case, I don't care. I'm listening to these songs—more like half-listening—sitting in my mother's car as she drives me to a home for unwed mothers.

Driving home one night in the spring of 1992, I found my favorite "oldies" station playing the top songs of early 1967. The memory of that seemingly endless drive twenty-five years before returned so powerfully that I had to stop along the road until I was no longer blinded by tears. In spite of the fact that I have written and stated publicly for years that I am grateful that the illegality of abortion helped to prevent me from destroying my son, I would be less than honest, if not hypocritical, if I did not also admit that the pain of giving him up for adoption has eaten at me spiritually and emotionally ever since. There have been days when the sense of loss was so overwhelming that I could almost understand what a woman in the mid-seventies once told me: she had aborted her child rather than put him up for adoption because, she said, "This way I know where he is."

But I say, "prevented me finally." Like many other young women in 1966 who found themselves pregnant and unmarried, my first thought was abortion. Typical American response: find the fastest, most complete way to deal with the problem and never mind the ethics of it. Like the stuff sold in the television commercials I grew up with—"a little dab'll do ya" and "plop, plop, fizz, fizz, oh what a relief it is"—abortion was an end-run around trouble, a panacea, a quick fix. A friend of mine in high school had an abortion in her senior year. She felt lousy for a few weeks afterwards, but the problem was solved, wasn't it?

Television commercials and rock and roll—that is what I remember of those years. If someone were to ask me what the bestselling book of the year was, I would not have a clue. I was indifferent to that element of the culture; I was reading books like James Joyce's *Ulysses* and books about Zen. Life in Dayton, Ohio was confining, frustrating: I felt I knew every painting in the Art Institute by heart. I attended concerts at the Philharmonic and plays at the handful of little theaters when I had the money. I even acted in summer stock productions of *South Pacific* and *My Fair Lady*, but my daydreams were fueled by memories of childhood visits to New York and San Francisco. My parents expected me to go to Miami University of Ohio and become a schoolteacher; I wanted to do anything *but* that.

A few years ago I read that when writers wanted to use a symbolic town to signify the real world, they would pick Dayton, Ohio. My hometown? I must have been missing something. During the Second World War, the General Motors and National Cash Register plants had drawn black and white laborers from all over the south, but by the mid-sixties no one could count any longer on a job at either plant and the civil rights movement had shattered Dayton's antebellum self-image of being a liberal town sympathetic to black aspirations. When my friend Leslie was found to be dating a black classmate in our senior year of high school, the full torrent of disapproval turned on her from our supposedly liberal community. My friends and I, thinking ourselves above the level of our high school classmates, sought refuge in occasional weekends at Antioch College, a small left-leaning school about thirty miles from Dayton. On one visit we saw a production of Archibald MacLeish's play *J. B.*, an adaptation of the Book of Job, and I was electrified; at seventeen, it was the first time I had ever seen the problem of suffering addressed. Although my parents refused to let me apply to Antioch (which was allegedly riddled with Communists), it was there that I met the boy who, after graduation from high school, fathered my child.

When I tumbled into my first sexual relationship in the summer of 1966, I had given very little thought to contraception. We weren't raised that way. On the third floor of my high school, where the science classrooms were, the health education teacher, who drove a beer truck in his spare time, taught us sex education. He showed us lurid color photos of human genitals pocked and festered by venereal disease, and said grimly, "Take it from me, I got six kids. Don't do it till you get married." We weren't sure whether to fear diseases or the act that transmitted them.

On the first floor, in the journalism room, things were different. In my senior year I was the newspaper editor with full command of the situation, since none of our teachers had the wits to keep us in control. We made *Playboy* our main course of study, and we drank deeply of its philosophy. Of course we claimed that reading *Playboy* was merely a journalistic pursuit and a learning experience: everyone knew it contained the best writing of any American magazine. Years later, when I used to hear people talking about how they only read *Playboy* for the excellence of its fiction and how misguided were the people who wanted to control its distribution, I could only shake my head in wonder. In 1966, in Dayton, Ohio, it was easy for high school students to get their hands on *Playboy* and we read it not for the fiction or the interviews, as we claimed, but for the shove it gave us toward the notion of "recreational sex."

My understanding of sex was deeply confused. Like most girls of my generation, I knew that a boy would tell any lie, make any promise, and hold out any hope to persuade a girl to have sex with him. Like most of the girls I knew as well, I had only the vaguest notion of what happened in the act or what might result from it. The notion that sex could be anything but painful and humiliating was drastically changed; thanks to my *Playboy* education, I came to believe that the act could not be anything less than ecstatic—unless one were "frigid," or a lesbian. Furthermore, most of us believed that sexual intercourse that occurred with both partners standing up could not result in pregnancy. My boyfriend's refusal to stand up or to use a condom (far more available in those days than people were willing to admit, but rarely considered) resulted, in my case, in pregnancy. I've never forgotten his excuse about the condom: he said it was "like kissing through a mask." I do not remember his excuse about not standing up.

When I realized I was pregnant, I was a college freshman in Indianapolis, away from home and the familiar network that could have located the abortionist my high-school classmate went to. Instead I listened to the usual "Everybody knows that" remedies for pregnancy: one night I ran desperately between hot and cold showers trying to cause a miscarriage, and another day I took a quantity of quinine and aspirin, which was rumored to induce abortion. Finally I told my roommate.

During our first week of rooming together Lina, a sophomore, had introduced me to Simone de Beauvoir's *The Second Sex* and the word "feminist." Desperate and frightened, I confided in her, hoping she would be on the right grapevine and able to direct me to the local abortionist. But Lina, as it happened, was a lesbian and connected to a different grapevine, so her response was to take me to a gay bar and urge me to drown my sorrows. No one knew about fetal alcohol syndrome in 1966 and I had never been to a bar, gay or otherwise; the prospect was wickedly exciting. I enjoyed the drag queen who performed, and I loved all the concern and attention that Lina's friends lavished on me, but when I got back to the dorm I wasn't any closer to getting rid of this nuisance, this embarrassment, this baby.

Eventually an older graduate student, a woman I met through Lina, gave me the name of two doctors, one of whom was suspected of doing abortions and the other known to for sure. The former was a gynecologist with an office in a posh neighborhood, so naturally I went there first. I guess I thought it would be safer. But the doctor fenced with me. I paid twenty-five dollars—a fortune for a college student in those days—for a pelvic exam and some tantalizing hints, but no promises. Running low on money, I decided to visit the second doctor, a general practitioner with an office in a run-down neighborhood. His waiting room was filled with poor people: old men with canes, anxious women holding feverish children, middle-aged women with thick ankles or fidgety hands. When I finally went in to see him, he struck me as a broken man. He sized me up pretty fast, denied that he did abortions, then told me to come back in a week at dinnertime with two hundred dollars in small bills.

My boyfriend immediately came to visit. He was as confused as I was, but convinced that abortion was the answer—whereas I wasn't. There was a large and elegant garden at one end of my college campus where we went for a walk to discuss my situation. He kept pressuring me about an abortion, and I kept asking him not to talk so loudly. Finally he stood on the crest of a small hill in the garden and shouted *"Abortion!"* at the top of his lungs. Other people were walking around in the gardens, and turned and looked at us; I wanted to die with shame. I told him to send me the money and I would go ahead with the abortion, which pleased him. The money arrived along with a letter in which he told me to "transcend the bourgeois," which meant, I suppose, have the abortion.

On the same day another letter arrived, this time from my best friend at high school. She also went to Antioch College and there she had heard I was contemplating an abortion. "Don't do this," Hannah wrote. "It's murder." Just like that: *it's murder.* We had known each other since we were eight, been in the Brownies and gone to ballet class together; she had loved Shelley's poetry in high school and had introduced me to the Romantics. Since she had also introduced me to my boyfriend on one of my visits to her, Hannah felt she had some responsibility for helping me cope with my pregnancy. So when the only daughter of a Jewish-Communist couple who had been blacklisted said to me, "It's murder," my heart missed a beat. My eighteen-year-old reasoning went like this: "If it's illegal, and *she* thinks it's murder, it's probably not a good thing and I'd better not do it."

I wandered around for a couple of days, torn between my fear of telling my parents and my fear of the broken-down doctor in his shabby office, while Hannah's words sounded in my heart. There was no sudden clarity, no blinding flash. I simply came to know that I could not do it. I took my boyfriend's money and bought maternity clothes and a bus ticket home. It was the first week in December. I felt hopeless. I had no idea how my parents would react; for myself, I had gone beyond despair. I look back and see myself operating half on instinct, half on a power that came from outside me and that I could only recognize in retrospect. I wanted something: love, or help, or an escape route. I did not know.

One of the last things I did before I told my parents was to tell my old boyfriend from high school. We had carried on a stormy relationship that was half-friendship, half-love affair from sophomore year on. In our senior year the relationship finally exploded. But that weekend, he was home and he took me out to dinner. When I told him my story, he made an extraordinary offer: if my parents threw me out, he would marry me. I thanked him and entertained some momentary misty fantasies, but I knew I would never take him up on it. The screaming rages we had enacted in the halls of our high school, throwing books and spite, gave me a pretty clear idea of what a marriage to him would be like.

The father of my baby had been another difficult character, though his behavior was less volatile—a nice enough guy as long as I didn't make the mistake of arguing with him about how thick a pizza crust should be, or whether Beethoven was better than Mozart. My pregnancy had brought out a strange new streak in him: he told me that if he married me and I moved to Antioch to live with him, I could just wear nightgowns while I was pregnant. "I can't wear nightgowns in public," I protested. "Totally bourgeois," he replied triumphantly. A life with him seemed a much poorer prospect than life with my old high school boyfriend. Miserable, I faced the fact that what I had thought in both cases to be true love was a mixture of glands, loneliness, intellectual isolation, and the adolescent girl's fascination with romance as a thing in itself. We wanted to get our periods, we wanted to have boyfriends, we wanted to get married, although what possible use any of those things were I no longer knew. I wondered briefly if maybe lesbians didn't have it better, being able to do without men. No matter about that now. If my parents threw me out, I was going to have to go it alone.

I had no concrete reason for assuming my parents would throw me out; if I had been thinking clearly, I would have realized that the evidence was all on the other side. During my senior year in high school, two girls in my class and one girl in the junior class all became pregnant. One of the girls in my class had an abortion; the other two had carried their babies to term and given them up for adoption. I did not tell my mother about the friend who had the abortion, but she knew all about the two other pregnancies from her best friend, the high school secretary. Both of the pregnant girls were required to leave school as soon as the pregnancy became visible, and I recall complaining to my mother how unfair it was that the boys in question went unpunished. My mother had nothing to say to that, which was unusual for her as she generally had an opinion on everything, but maybe she knew something I didn't. In any case her attitude toward the girls was not punitive, although she thought they should not be living at home.

Still, I hesitated, because my parents both tended to be somewhat erratic. What I said or did one day that would amuse or interest them would on another day make them angry. My father was an intelligent, independent-minded man who chafed at having to work for others. Throughout my childhood, he threw himself into one get-rich-quick scheme after another in order to secure an income for us without having a boss, but none of them worked. My mother was a gifted artist who had been prevented from taking an art scholarship in 1944 because my grandmother insisted that she go to work in a defense factory; they had been desperately poor in the Depression and the temptation of regular factory wages was great. But when the war was over it was too late: my mother met my dad, married, I was born a year later,

· ·

and the sketchpads went into a bottom drawer and were forgotten. I did not feel sorry for my parents then. I do now.

When I told my parents that I was pregnant they did not throw me out, but they were not the least bit happy about the news I brought them. I told my mother first, alone, in my bedroom. Whatever she might have felt or thought about it she did not express, but her thin, stiff lips and set jaw gave me the horrible feeling that she had suspected all along that something like this would happen. Without much comment she took me out to tell my father, who called me a whore and then stormed around the house until he had worn himself out. When they got over being furiously angry and disgusted, which took about twenty-four hours, my parents cried and hugged me and tried to help me figure out what to do. My father made noises about the father of the baby and marriage, but I was certain that I wanted to give the baby up for adoption and return to college. With the help of an adoption agency, my parents located the Catherine Booth Hospital and Residence in a nearby city, where I went to live not long after Christmas.

During the Christmas break, I told all my friends. My parents would have been appalled had they known. We had supposedly agreed that no one was to know except my grandmother. What that meant is that my parents insisted that I tell no one that I was pregnant, and as always in my relationship with them, I chose discretion as the better part of valor and mumbled something that signified assent. My former boyfriend, my best friend, and my former roommate all knew anyway, and I had no illusions that any of them would refrain from telling one or two people more—in complete confidence, of course. As far as my high school friends were concerned, I might as well be frank with them about my situation because I knew most certainly that they would hear the story at some point. Best they heard it from the source. Nobody really seemed to care much about what had happened to me, or else they were too embarrassed to talk about it. One evening I simply said, "Listen, everybody, I've got bad news, I'm pregnant," and the response was, "Really? Are you craving pickles and ice cream? Hey, there's a thought! Let's go out for ice cream!"

But one element of my story did get a response: my friends were almost all shocked that my grandmother knew. My mother's mother was, in many ways, my closest confidante; she had cared for me since I was little, while my parents worked, and now once more she was going to care for me. I went to live with her from after Christmas until the end of January when I would move to the Catherine Booth Home. This stratagem was thought up to keep me under cover locally so that other family and neighbors and friends would not suspect that I was not in college. Additionally, Grandma had a very long driveway and I could be safely hidden in the back bedroom before any unexpected visitor reached the front door.

It is hard for people nowadays to imagine the degree of shame that could accompany an unwed pregnancy in a working-class midwestern family in 1966. I remember those two girls from my high school who were pregnant: both of them stayed at home for the duration, but they rarely went out. The mother of the girl who was younger than I, whom my mother knew through the P.T.A., stopped answering her phone. One day close to graduation I ran into the girl from my class in the front hall of our high school. She was crouched over and tiptoeing, like a bad actress playing a spy. I started to greet her, but she only glanced at me, placed her finger to her lips, and crept away. For my parents, there was a strong element of disappointment as well. I was the first person in my mother's family, and only the second in my father's, to go to college. To admit I had wasted this opportunity through illicit sex was unthinkable.

Discouraged but unshaken, my grandmother had readily agreed that I stay with her. Once I arrived, she craftily planned trips to Big Boy restaurants and shopping centers in distant towns to counter my cabin fever and to nourish her own love of food and shopping. I pierced her ears, and we shopped for earrings all over three states. I convinced her to join me in watching the vampire soap opera *Dark Shadows*, a college favorite, and she could count on me to keep her company with the *Ruth Lyons Show*—an Ohio specialty starring a white Oprah Winfrey—just as I had done as a child. Together we spent a month in Never-Never Land.

I emerged from that dream world on two brief occasions. One was New Year's Day, when I went to the movie *Alfie* with my high school friends. During that movie I first felt my baby move, and first saw and heard an abortion discussed in public. In the movie abortion was represented as the cruel tidying-up of a woman's unruly body, demanded by a selfish and sadistic man, and it caused me to weep. It would be years before I could feel that grateful again that I had not ended the life that was growing in me. The other occasion was a visit by two boys I had been friends with in college, a visit that grew awkward and embarrassing as they realized why I wasn't in school any more. I realized I preferred the indifference of most of my high school friends; I was glad when they left.

I was nobody's idea of a Christian, but in my solitude I was spending a lot of time trying to pray. My idea of prayer in those days was a combination of memorized prayers from childhood and the "laundry list" approach, which consisted of telling God what to do in case he couldn't figure it out by himself. It was rarely consoling or reassuring; prayer was like standing in an empty room talking to myself. Yet I felt I had to do it. There was nobody else around, after all, to hear the anxious pleadings of my heart. My grandmother was her usual placid, rather greedy self, and my parents were having increasing difficulty coping with my situation. My father had become almost morbidly solicitous, taking me shopping for a new coat and gloves. "What can I do?" he asked my grandmother and my mother, "what can I do?" My mother became equally preoccupied with what she thought of as my sex life, but after she had arrived at my grandparents' house twice in one week to interrogate me about how I got pregnant, my grandfather threw her out in a fury. What did she think, he demanded, she would accomplish by that, for herself or for me? As January wore on, prayer gradually dwindled to a desperate repetition of the Jesus Prayer, which I had learned from reading J. D. Salinger's *Franny and Zooey*. It was the only thing I had to keep my head above water.

What a relief, then, when I finally went to spend the rest of my pregnancy at the Catherine Booth Hospital and Residence, named for the co-founder of the Salvation Army. The Salvation

Army was beyond the narrow range of my exposure to Christianity. My entire knowledge of the Salvation Army consisted of men with red kettles ringing bells on streetcorners near Christmas, and a goofy little ditty that my friends and I sang:

> Oh, when I was sixteen I was the village belle,
> But the life that I was leading, I was headed straight for hell.
> I rode a tandem bicycle, my ankles were in view,
> Then came the glorious Army, and I was born anew.

When I went to be interviewed at Catherine Booth, however, the woman who spoke to my mother and me was a Jewish social worker. A black nurse, identified as Captain somebody or other, took me out of the interview at a certain point to give me a brief physical exam, but she was dressed as a nurse and was cheerful and kind, not fanatical or in uniform. Thus I arrived at my new home with a few books and clothes, some shampoo and writing paper, a Joan Baez poster for my wall, a cheap record player, and a couple of records. I had no idea what I would find or who I would meet—all I knew was that the emotional exhaustion of being around my family and friends was too great. My baby kicked and bounced in my womb, and there was no one I could tell. He and I were alone, and I desperately needed a friend to whom I could say, "I'm frightened, I'm so lonely, what is going to happen to me?"

TWO

The Catherine Booth Hospital and Residence was located in a black neighborhood in Cincinnati. It provided inpatient maternity care, outpatient prenatal and well-baby care, and a residential unit for girls and women awaiting birth. I was about four-and-a-half months pregnant when I went there, which was average. Some girls arrived at two or three months pregnant—their parents were taking no chances. It made the older girls and women angry when a girl of fourteen or fifteen would show up when she was still suffering from morning sickness and Dorothy, a rotund widow in her late thirties, would go to the bathrooms and help the sick ones. Later she would say, "If it was my kid, I wouldn't leave her alone to go through this."

I don't think there were more than two dozen girls and women in residence. I remember the group as small and connected, if not uniformly friendly. During my stay they ranged from age eleven to late thirties, with the majority being about sixteen to twenty-two. The first two inmates I met were Barb and Kate, who were rather like prefects and assigned to show new girls around. All the pregnant residents were referred to generically as "girls," no matter what our age, and those who worked there were generically "staff," whether volunteer, cook, or doctor. We girls referred to ourselves as the "pregnant mommies" in defiance of the tendency to secrecy and euphemism that was part of the Catherine Booth ethos.

The Salvation Army understood the shame that was associated in those days with illegitimate pregnancy, and while it would not be fair to say they exploited it, neither did they make any real effort to overcome it. Our last names were hidden from each other, but nothing prevented girls who became friends from divulging names and hometowns to one another. Staff, whether secular or Army, never condemned us; in fact, they urged us to believe in God's love for us. On the other hand, the restrictions on visitors, movement, mail, telephone calls, and television suggested an almost medieval suspicion of contamination by the outside world. We had two free days a week: Wednesday and Saturday. On Wednesday those of us who were over eighteen could leave after lunch, unsupervised, and we did not have to be back until dinner at five p.m. We did not have to say where we were going; we only had to sign out. The rules for girls under eighteen were stricter: they had to have their plans approved and they could not travel alone. On Saturday we could leave after breakfast if we were going somewhere with family; otherwise we could leave after lunch again only by signing out.

Catherine Booth was in a pleasant, if poor, residential neighborhood, but a small shopping area and bus stops were a short walk away. We girls did have a certain freedom in the neighborhood. Our faces—my one black friend, Angela, rarely went out for fear of encountering someone she knew—and those of the white members of the staff were the only regularly-appearing white faces for blocks, so when we went for walks or to have coffee or ice cream at the small, painfully tidy diner nearby, everyone knew who we were, and we were accepted. The man who kept the shoe repair shop stood in his doorway on Wednesday afternoons when the weather was good and greeted us as we walked by. We belonged there, and even in the tense spring before the burning of Detroit and Newark in the race riots of 1967, white Catherine Booth girls walked easily in this black neighborhood.

Unquestioning obedience to the rules—a major tenet of Salvation Army discipline—was expected of us just as it was of Army members. Yet if we were potential converts or objects of rescue, we never realized it. Our treatment was morally strict and spiritually gentle. If I had been told that someone was trying to convert me, I would have been surprised to hear it.

Barb and Kate, who showed me around when I first arrived, shared one of the two two-bedded rooms in the residential area; all the rest of the rooms were four-bedded. They had arrived at Catherine Booth within days of one another near the end of their fourth month and claimed this two-bedded room soon after. Barb was small and compact, with a puffy face and sad eyes. Kate was tall and had cascades of thick, wavy blonde hair which Barb, a hairdresser by profession, experimented on regularly. They kept illegal chocolates in their room and were suspected of smoking as well. They had sewn curtains and coverlets; there were tasteful prints on the walls and a couple of coordinating throw-pillows on an overstuffed chair scavenged from somewhere. Their space, they told me, had been made as much as possible like rooms they would want to live in at home. There were three old but highly functional treadle sewing machines in the basement, they explained. Barb and Kate had sewed not only curtains but clothes as well, and offered to let me use their patterns.

They were also the leaders of one of the two factions among the girls. The two factions were basically divided into the girls who went to "the smoker"—a small, cramped room that was the only place where cigarette smoking was permitted in the building—and those who didn't. Barb and Kate did not, and they clearly looked down on those who did. Rumors that they smoked illegally in their room may have been revenge on the part of the smokers or it may have been due to the fact that their window was always open, even in February. When Barb took me around the building, she pointed out the smoker with obvious distaste. "That's where you have to go to smoke," she said, as if she were describing a charnelhouse. I came to realize that Barb was a very fastidious young woman.

The leaders of the other faction were as mismatched as Barb and Kate were similar. Dorothy, the widow, and Louisa, a girl of twelve, were the staples of the smoker contingent. I can still see their faces: it strikes me as odd that they should seem so similar in recollection. Round faces, big hair, the sprouting bellies that embarrassed me in those early days, almost as if I'd never seen pregnant women before. Dorothy was a robust, earthy mother of six who had sought consolation after her husband's death and wound up pregnant. Her family was under the impression that she was undergoing treatment in Arizona for tuberculosis, for in those days people still went to tuberculosis sanitariums, just as teenaged girls still went to homes for unwed mothers.

Twelve-year-old Louisa became a ward of the court of the state of Kentucky after she was found to be pregnant and had no idea whether her father, her brother, or one of her two uncles was responsible. She was a child, but there was not much of childhood left in her. She had been used sexually by the men in her family as long as she could remember; now she sat and smoked angrily, regaling every new resident with the details of her abuse. On the first of my two visits to the smoker—I did not smoke but was trying to get to know people—Louisa told me her story, tapping her long blood-red fingernails on the table beside her to emphasize her points.

"They did this to me," she said bitterly, "and they're out there, and I'm locked up. I didn't commit a crime, they did. But those bastards are free, and I'm locked up."

"C'mon, honey," Dorothy would say. I came to understand that this was a common exchange between them. "Calm down. God'll get 'em, just you wait. 'Vengeance is mine, I will repay,' thus says the Lord.'"

"I wanna see it," Louisa would reply through clenched teeth. "I wanna see them pay."

Perhaps one of the reasons that some of us avoided the smoker was the power of Louisa's rage. It was not an easy thing to experience. Louisa had spent her whole short life assuming that the brutal treatment she had experienced was normal; when she arrived at Catherine Booth and began talking to other girls and found it was not, her shame and anger were endless. There was no use in telling her it was not her fault. She wanted revenge, and she was clear about what that meant. No Roman centurion tossing Christians to the lions could have done so with a clearer sense of the fitness of the punishment.

Clare, a resident who later became a close friend of mine after we both left, once said to Louisa, "It would have been better if you could have had an abortion." Louisa's outrage could not be contained. "I'm not killing this baby!" she shrieked. "I want to kill the men who did this to me! It's not the baby's fault. I don't want it, but you leave it *alone*. It's not the baby's fault!"

Clare and I puzzled over this outburst. It was not until years later that we began to see that Louisa's moral clarity was in some ways more developed than ours. She felt that she knew who had done wrong and who had not, and she was as unwilling to forgive the guilty as she was to punish the innocent. Louisa made everyone miserable, including herself, yet the purity of her pain and rage was so clear and focused that I have never been able to remove her face and her words from my memory.

I knew nothing in those days of the Salvation Army's history of social radicalism. Catherine Booth, for whom the home was named, was an Englishwoman who had co-founded the Salvation Army with her husband William in 1865. She had been influenced by an American Holiness theologian named Phoebe Palmer, who believed that a woman who had been sanctified by the Holy Spirit was not only free to preach and minister, but in fact called to do both. Consequently, in the founding of the Salvation Army, sexual equality in leadership was one of its features. As a preacher and an advocate for women and the poor, Catherine Booth was and remains an unsung heroine of early feminism. The Booths' work in the nineteenth and early twentieth centuries in reclaiming prostitutes led to the establishment of places like the residence in Cincinnati where I lived.

Alongside the experience of living in an interracial environment was the experience of an institution that was free of a formal sexual hierarchy. The head of the hospital and residence was a high-ranking woman Salvation Army officer; the staff doctors, a Chicano man (Dr. Jay) and a woman of Filipino descent (Dr. Lee). I had never known a woman doctor before in my life. The supervising nurses were both black women: the outpatient head was the Salvation Army captain I met at my intake interview;

the inpatient head was a willowy beauty who was very pregnant with her own first child when I left. A black and a white nurse shared responsibility for the nursery, while two white nurses were the mainstays of the delivery room. Few girls were allowed on the hospital floor, but we became acquainted with the hospital personnel in the lunchroom we all shared.

We all had workjobs, and mine was in the kitchen under a troika of strong black women. Even the white dietician with her college degree submitted to their sway, yet I was stunned when a young male Salvation Army recruit who arrived to assist for a few weeks also bent to the rule of these women with both humility and cheerfulness. He was not much older than I was, yet he stood for hours scrubbing large and crusted-over pots without complaint. That made him unlike any other male I'd ever known. Even my father, who agreed to do the vacuuming at home, recoiled from dishwashing. The recruit and the hospital bookkeeper were the only two Anglo-Saxon males I saw on a regular basis, although the Salvation Army chaplains who came to lead our worship services were also men. But outside the Sunday and Wednesday chapel services, we did not see much of them.

On the "girls' side" black and white women lived together. Period. It was unusual for the mid-sixties, but I considered myself very much the liberal and supported the civil rights movement. At Catherine Booth I met Angela, my first black friend and a woman a year older than I whose plump, sweet face hid a wicked sense of humor. She was a student at Spelman College in Atlanta, and already in residence when I arrived and was assigned to her room. We became friends one Saturday when Angela had no one but me to help her iron her hair. The other black resident at Catherine Booth was tall and aloof; her major contact with Angela was in regard to the mysteries of straightening, ironing, and otherwise contending with unruly, pre-Afro hair.

Many other black girls and women from the neighborhood went through the outpatient clinic, but we residents had little or no contact with them. Barb and Kate told me that two black women in the home at once was unusual. There had been none when either of them arrived; from what they had heard from girls who were there before them, only a handful of black women were thought to have lived at Catherine Booth at all. Barb and Kate also admitted that they were initially upset by having to live next door to "colored," as they put it. They were both from southern Indiana and trying hard to be decent, but they had grown up in a segregated world, and the unquestioning interracial living of the residence—also basic to the Salvation Army way of doing things—unsettled them.

Angela's and my room was a four-bedded one. One of our other roommates was a tall, cadaverous blonde from Kentucky who seemed to be personally acquainted with the residents of every mental institution in her home state and regaled us with stories about them. "There's a man in the state asylum in Louisville," she insisted, "who smokes two hundred Salem cigarettes a day. He has nearly burned that asylum down three times. I do not know why they let him go on smoking those Salem cigarettes." Angela and I learned fast not to argue with her, and to contain our giggles until we got outside. I don't remember the fourth person; whoever she was, she was soon replaced by Terry.

Terry was one of those whose parents weren't taking any chances. She arrived right at the end of her third month and came from the kind of family for which the notions of secrecy and isolation of the residence were designed. We were required to go by our first names and last initial, as in Alcoholics Anonymous. When our mail came, the last name on the envelope—and often the return address—had been blotted out in the office. Terry's family sent her copies of the hometown newspaper with the name of the town carefully cut away or scratched out on every page. She had been in college but wouldn't say where. She was friendly but reserved; pretty, but somewhat washed out and fragile. Angela liked her, but called her "the ghost."

Our tall Kentuckian disappeared about two weeks after I arrived. She did not literally disappear; she went into labor and was transferred to the other side to give birth. There were two sections to the building that contained the hospital and residence: one wing contained the girls' residence, some classrooms, offices, and meeting rooms, and the senior administrator's apartment; this was called the "girls' side." The other wing had the outpatient clinic on the main floor, plus more offices, the kitchens, and the cafeteria for girls and staff. The second floor of this wing was the hospital, including labor rooms, pharmacy, nursery, and delivery room, and it was off-limits to us except in specific and limited circumstances—one of which was, obviously, giving birth. Down the hall from my bedroom was a broad set of double doors that led to the "hospital side," but it might as well have been a brick wall with barbed wire atop it. The sign on the door read *Hospital—authorized personnel only.* We were not allowed through that door; we were not even allowed to see anyone again once she had delivered her baby. Dante could not have envisioned so complete a separation between heaven and hell.

Yet somehow I wound up over there and saw our Kentucky roommate once more. I may have been sent to deliver a message; in any case one of the nurses turned a blind eye while I slipped into the woman's room and asked her how she was. She complained that her episiotomy stitches hurt: "Mah stitches eee-yich," she said miserably. She looked a little less haggard than before the birth and asked me to tell everyone it isn't so bad after all. I slipped away again, feeling I had broached a great mystery. Angela was delighted by my coup; Terry looked nervous but decided, after some wrestling with herself, that since I'd been on the hospital floor with permission it was almost the same as being allowed to go visit our ex-roommate.

The Kentuckian was replaced by another blonde, who arrived with a broad grin and a guitar. Her name was Clare, and she was to be my friend for many years after we left Catherine Booth. With her arrival our room almost immediately took on the ambience of a college dorm. I had the record player and she had the guitar and Angela had the secret store of junk food. Terry was ambivalent about this libertine state of affairs. Clare and Angela and I decided that if we were going to have to be there for four more months—actually Clare, like Terry, was looking at nearly five months until her due date—we were going to make the best of it, but I think Terry wanted us to practice a more penitential attitude. "I mean, after all, you guys, we're here because we're in trouble."

Angela wouldn't have any part of it. "I bet my boyfriend's not moping around, and I don't intend to either."

Clare, a natural anarchist, would have no part in the factions between the smoker crowd and the non-smokers. She made a conscious effort to befriend everyone and although she did not smoke, she made a point of visiting the smoker for at least a few minutes each day. As a result she was not considered stuck-up like Angela and Terry and me, and by being in good with the smoker crowd, she was privvy to the juiciest gossip. Additionally, Clare's workjob turned out to be delivering lunch and dinner to the patients on hospital side, so she found herself much sought after as a source of information about the duration of labors, the appearance of babies, and the dresses worn home by the newly flat-tummied. Angela, Terry, and I basked in her reflected glory.

The staff at Catherine Booth included social workers. I only knew two of them: one a Jewish woman assigned to me and the other a black man who was reputed to be a champion at storming the welfare system to get money for girls like Louisa. Since I was not on welfare and had normal—given the circumstances—relations with my parents, the only task the social worker had to undertake with me was the ever-thorny and painful question of the degree of contact I would have with my baby after birth.

Our possibilities were limited, but each was a potential source of grief. The first choice was to give birth under general anaesthesia and never see the child at all. The second possibility, if the doctor approved, was to deliver with a spinal block and see the child only at birth, but not again. Or one could observe the birth and later look at the baby in the nursery. The nursery nurses were informed which girls had chosen to see their babies during the viewing hours and they were trusted for their discretion. The possibilities of holding one's child and feeding it were mentioned but not encouraged. And would we name our babies? A racist rumor circulated that the black nurses would name otherwise unnamed babies—usually with names like Roosevelt and Franklin. Clare investigated and quietly but firmly repudiated this. Several meetings with the social worker were usually required to solve these dilemmas, and although many of the younger girls' parents insisted that the girl have no contact with her infant, the social workers generally tended to be sympathetic to the parents and then allow the girl, if she was over eighteen, to make her own decision once the parents were gone.

Hanging over the entire topic, like a thundercloud on a late August afternoon, was the possibility of keeping the baby. It was discussed in hushed conversations with one's closest friends. If a girl voiced the idea that *perhaps*... the word ran like electricity through the gossip circuits. *She's thinking about keeping the baby!* The girl in question would suddenly be surrounded with a kind of aura, an element of mystery, a fearful expectation. If the word hit the staff, which it usually did, the girl could be sure to be sent for by Captain Green, the no-nonsense-but-a-heart-of-gold head outpatient nurse. Captain Green would describe the hard realities of single motherhood that she saw every day in the well-baby clinic, and urge the girl to evaluate carefully the degree to which family and friends could be expected to be supportive. At a time when very little good day care was available and the social stigma of unwed motherhood was still severe, the longing to keep the baby was not difficult to overcome, given the bleakness of the life most girls faced if they succumbed.

Terry, who was my age, had been ordered by her parents to take the general anaesthesia and not see the child. She agonized over it, wanting desperately to be obedient and wanting just as desperately to see her child. She was, I believe, one of the few girls to request a meeting with one of the chaplains to sort out her decision. For Terry it was a religious question, a question of obedience to her parents, as the fifth commandment implied. She said little about their conversations—I seem to recall there were several—but in the end she acquiesced to her parents' wishes. Angela, Clare, and I watched her struggle in near silence during this period, but didn't know what to say. Our parents had all told us to decide for ourselves.

For Angela and the other black woman, the agonizing had a different and more compelling edge. They were not particularly interested in keeping their babies, although they felt that the black community tended to be less harsh on girls in their situation than white families were. Angela's friend was a singer in a "girl group" that had scored some successes in clubs and cafes around southern Ohio and she was eager to get on with her career. Angela intended to finish Spelman and go into politics (every time I see an article about a black woman politician I look carefully at the photo to see if it might be her). They were both ambitious and knew that child-raising was not a good thing for them at the time.

On the other hand they were black, and adoption placement for black infants was tough. They also had to decide whether they could permit white families to adopt their babies. One week Angela would say, "Better a white family than a lifetime in foster care." The next week she would change her mind: "I want my child to grow up black and proud. No white family could do that." The singer finally decided to permit a white placement. Up to her due date, Angela had been unable to decide, in spite of hearing from the social workers that there were no black couples currently seeking infants. Finally she too permitted a white placement, and cried bitterly after she signed the form. If I had ever thought that race relations in America could be easily transformed by some laws and everyone trying to be nice to each other, Angela's agony disabused me of that forever.

Angela's pain was not the only kind of pain, nor was hers the only courage. Mary Margaret's situation was as terrible in its own way. Barb had delivered her baby a month ahead of schedule, and her abruptly-vacated twin bed was assigned to a handsome, gregarious woman in her mid-twenties named Mary Margaret. She was in some kind of business that required international travel, which enthralled small-town Ohio girls like Clare and Terry and me. But if Mary Margaret's work sounded thrilling, the story of her pregnancy was the stuff of movies.

She was of Irish descent, first generation, I think, and when her job took her to Ireland she was able to extend her time, take some vacation, and visit the place her parents had come from. In their hometown she met a man and it was love at first sight. Michael was acquainted with her relatives, and for several days he was her constant companion. Before she left Ireland, he proposed. She accepted and flew back to Pittsburgh sporting a sizeable diamond. Her parents were ecstatic. She was ecstatic.

Mary Margaret and Michael corresponded and talked on the phone for several weeks, and then he came to visit. Her parents were charmed, not only because he was wealthy and handsome, but because he was from "the auld sod" and a devout Roman Catholic who went to Mass every morning. Mary Margaret dug out the rosary she'd put away once she'd finished Catholic high school and trotted off to early Mass daily with her Michael, fervently praying her beads. The wedding date was set. Michael left a pile of traveler's checks to cover Mary Margaret's visit to Ireland a month later to meet his parents.

While she was on the plane, her father received a letter from his cousin back in Ireland. Michael, it seems, was already married. His wife had either run off with another man, joined a cult somewhere in India, or—the cousin thought this the most likely—been committed to a mental institution. The cousin had heard Michael was talking about marrying this American girl and then moving to America and getting a divorce from the first wife (impossible in Ireland), after which he would do the right thing and marry Mary Margaret properly. Michael really did love her, the cousin assured Mary Margaret's father. It was just these priest-ridden laws in Ireland....

It was as well for Michael that Mary Margaret's father was an ocean away and not rich enough to buy a ticket for the first plane to Shannon. When she called to tell her parents she'd arrived, her father broke the news to her, brutally. He told her to get on the next plane home. She tearfully confronted Michael and he admitted it was true. His wife had run away a few years earlier with a man; she had returned home months later frightened and incoherent. Time and patience did not bring improvement; finally he'd had her committed for her own safety. The doctors speculated the seducer was some kind of Bluebeard and that the woman had barely escaped with her life. Yes, Michael admitted, he was still married to her, but what kind of marriage was it now? No marriage at all, and he despaired of getting an annulment from the Roman Catholic Church. His only hope was an American divorce, but he couldn't get an American divorce until he was resident in America. They would have to have one sham marriage and then one real one. Could she trust him?

Mary Margaret didn't know. She had to think. She kissed Michael good-bye, gave back his ring, and returned to Pittsburgh. Not long after she got home, she began throwing up. She thought it was "nerves." Several more weeks passed before she realized that one of those mornings before Mass, while her parents slept, she and Michael had made a baby.

Now her father's wrath knew no bounds. He made noises about going to Ireland to kill Michael. Michael, meanwhile, wrote almost daily, pleading with Mary Margaret to come to him. Somehow they would brave it out. Somehow they would make it work. Somehow.

But her early training held, and Mary Margaret went with her mother to the parish priest. She showed him all of Michael's letters and he read and fretted, and fretted and read. Finally the priest said sadly, "If you do what this man asks, you will suffer shipwreck in the faith," and Mary Margaret, by her own admission, broke down. That phrase, *suffer shipwreck in the faith*, stuck with me; two decades later I found it in a papal document defining the Immaculate Conception. I doubt that Mary Margaret knew where it came from; all she knew was she was pregnant and husbandless and without hope. The priest helped her find the Catherine Booth Residence, but she was into her seventh month before she arrived.

No sooner had she arrived than she took up her correspondence with Michael again. He continued to promise marriage as soon as he could leave his wife. He claimed he was working through the church for a proper annulment. Clare and I were romantically inclined and initially adored the whole idea of Mary Margaret's story; Kate, Angela, and Terry all disapproved, as did the now mightily pregnant Dorothy, who had, during my tenure, become the de facto pope of the girls' side. "Men are scum," Dorothy opined one evening when Mary Margaret had gone to bed. "The more I hear about 'em, the more I think they're scum." Angela agreed, from her own perspective: "Any black woman'll tell you, white men aren't worth the paper they're printed on."

But no one wanted to see Mary Margaret cry her huge, silent tears, her winsome face a mask of tragedy, so even Clare and I learned to keep quiet when we had second thoughts about

Michael's possibilities as a husband and father. Four months later, when Clare gave birth, Mary Margaret's little boy still lived, two months old, in the Catherine Booth nursery while Mary Margaret waited for Michael's hoped-for annulment. The nursery nurses were his mother and father. Whether he ever had any other, particularly the woman and man who had created him and wanted to marry and raise him, we never knew.

THREE

About the time I reached my sixth month of pregnancy, Catherine Booth started me on a comprehensive childbirth preparation course, beginning with a detailed explanation of sexual relations. We read of Abraham and Hagar and Sarah; we read of Tamar and Amnon; we read the Song of Solomon. Sex, I came to understand, was not something God hated and tried to repress; rather, it was something that God created and gave to human beings to experience and enjoy, albeit in an orderly fashion. When God's intentions for sexual expression were not honored, disaster followed. That part seemed pretty clearly demonstrated by our predicaments.

We learned about male and female anatomy and how they prepare for maturity, intercourse, and reproduction; we learned about the miracle of conception. We saw and held life-size plaster models of developing babies, and Captain Green, who was the main teacher of this class, continually stressed God's enormous love for us and for our babies. The stigma of illegitimacy had no place in her theology.

And yet, and yet, and yet. Back in our rooms, we talked about abortion. A few of us knew someone who had had one and our ambivalence was great. We felt our babies kick and somersault; we knew that there was a little living somebody within. Clare occasionally got to see an infant through the nursery window; once one of the nursery nurses brought a newborn to the window, held him up for Clare to see, and made his tiny fist wave hello. Clare came back to the room, shut the door, and cried. We knew our babies were real, were human, were alive. And yet, and yet, and yet. Had we had the chance, many of us, when our babies were smaller and more fragile and less distinctively human-looking, would have ended their lives. Why? For the same reason, perhaps, that an animal caught in a trap might chew off its own leg. Frightened, frustrated, angry people often cannot think through the moral and practical aspects of their situation.[1]

And very often, then as now, few people want to take the time and energy to sit down with a pregnant woman and help her think through her situation. So often the woman feels that she is alone and without resources, even if this is actually mistaken. Years later, when I was teaching at the University of Massachusetts, a pregnant girl came to me and said, "Of course I can't tell my parents." I swallowed hard and suggested that she try. I told her I'd told mine, years before, and although they were unhappy, they had supported me. She went to her parents, who indeed were unhappy, but who did help her have her baby and arrange an adoption. But what if I had said nothing?

Shame was another powerful impetus to abortion. Dorothy, a grown woman with a powerful personality, nevertheless could not bring herself to tell her children or her siblings that she had become pregnant within a few months of her husband's death. Clare was a minister's daughter, and even her brother and sister did not know that she wasn't in college. My parents were willing to go any distance, tell any lie, to conceal my grievous fault. Terry's parents carried shame into near paranoia with their cut-up newspapers: Clare reported to me long after we left Catherine Booth that Terry said her parents went to these extremes of secrecy out of fear of blackmail.

When I was well into my ninth month, Captain Green asked me to help her speak to a new arrival. The new arrival turned out to be a very young girl, not quite eleven, who looked like a child, was dressed as a child, and did not even have breasts as far as I could tell. Like Angela, she was from a middle-class black family. Unlike Angela, however, Lucy did not understand where she was or why she was there. She thought she was in reform school, and she kept pleading with Captain Green that she would be good if only she could go home. I don't think Captain Green called on me because I was particularly wise or friendly; I think she called on me because I was hugely pregnant. I was a visual aid.

Gently and carefully, Captain Green showed her my mound of belly and baby and explained what my condition was. She then explained to Lucy that she too was pregnant, and she was not in reform school, but in a home where people would take good care of her and her growing baby. Lucy was quiet for a moment, then asked how it got in there. The baby, she meant. She did not know what she had done to get pregnant.

Captain Green was apparently prepared for this part of the story. Lucy had a brother a few years older, and one of his friends had convinced the girl to play a game with him, and she did not quite understand it. Her parents had got this out of the brother when they discovered Lucy's condition. The brother had known what was going on, but had been kept silent either by bribes or threats, I don't remember which. The parents were apparently straitlaced people who could not cope with their daughter's disaster and had done nothing to explain to her what had happened to her or where she was going. All this they had dumped in Captain Green's lap.

In response to Captain Green's request, I told Lucy as simply as possible what I had done to get pregnant, and Lucy's eyes filled with tears. The attention that the older boy had paid her, which had seemed so wonderful to a naive child, was now revealed as a mean trick. Captain Green held the girl while she cried a little, then Lucy rallied and put on a brave face. We took her down to the kitchen and asked Jenny, the head cook, if some milk and cookies might be available. Jenny, who ran the kitchen with an iron hand and brooked no deviations from the rules, softened at the sight of poor Lucy. While Captain Green conferred with Jenny, I sat with the child while she had her snack and told her that all of us girls would be big sisters to her while she lived with us. She thought that would be nice, because she didn't have a big sister. From the kitchen I heard Captain Green's low voice, and then Jenny's "My, my, my, my, my!" This was a clue to me of how deeply concerned Jenny was. A woman of few words, her usual response to most things was, "Mmm." Anything that got more than "My, my," out of her was clearly an issue of earthshaking importance to her. The extremity of her reply to Captain Green signalled me that Jenny was deeply, profoundly disturbed, and that I had better be on my best behavior that evening in the kitchen.

Louisa had long since delivered her baby, and Angela was gone too. With some hushed conversation and scurrying about, Clare and I tried to get a sense of what the girls would like to do about rooming with Lucy. Something else I discovered at Catherine Booth was the power of community. If we could figure out a way to do what we felt was right, we could usually do it. It took a little guts, a little sneakiness, and a few carefully chosen words to certain members of the staff. Ninety-nine times out of a hundred we pulled it off. And in all fairness, I think the staff respected this kind of democratic effort.

So it happened with our concern about Lucy. A sad-faced woman of nineteen or so said she'd be willing to share a room with the girl, as she had several younger sisters and was used to little kids. By now Kate and Mary Margaret were both discharged, and their two-bedded room stood empty. Clare and I had thought to claim it, but now we said we were too lazy to move. The sad-faced young woman was a rape victim, the only girl at Catherine Booth who ever described herself that way to me. As I look back on it, I am guessing that she felt a certain kinship with Lucy. All the rest of us (except Louisa, of course, who was gone) had been morally complicit in the act that conceived our babies.

Today, when someone tells me that I ought at least to accept abortion as the lesser of two evils in cases of rape or child abuse, I tend to say that the victims of a crime should not be punished, and to abort a baby because its father was a criminal means that one of the innocent parties suffers the death penalty. Louisa's rage always stopped before that point. What about another victimized mother's suffering? It is certainly suffering, but pregnancy and death are neither legal nor moral equivalents. Would earlier sex education or easily available birth control have helped Lucy? Certainly her parents' inability to talk to her about sex left her vulnerable to her brother's predatory friend. But if Lucy had known and understood what he was up to, I doubt that she would have wanted birth control; she would have wanted protection from the friend himself. As it turned out, Lucy went into labor prematurely and gave birth to a pathetic premature infant who lived but a few hours. Today I suppose most people would say that such an outcome was "for the best," but I can't remember ever hearing anyone say in 1967 that the death of a child was for the best.

At Catherine Booth, Christian teachings and Christian values were emphasized in every way, but in an experiential rather than dogmatic fashion. I never felt judged or condemned, but loved and forgiven. A guest preacher one Sunday morning used Matthew's gospel of the birth of Jesus for his text, pointing out that Joseph was about to send Mary away, but an angel intervened. In her own culture Mary would have been treated as we were, and probably worse—she could have been stoned to death. Jesus' mother was like us, he said.

While we suffered little or no blame for our predicament, discipline at Catherine Booth was still a serious issue. The rules for girls were simple and clear: all ten commandments were enforced. Lying, blasphemy, and theft were treated with equal seriousness, and enduring the impassioned exhortations of Brigadier Smith, the administrator, or Captain Green, or one of the chaplains was almost worse than a flogging. First and even second offenses were treated with lectures and the loss of a free day or two. I endured a lecture once, and swore to myself I would never face it again. During my stay, only one person had to be sent away. Her name was Gloria and she had violated the one rule that was definitely not based on the ten commandments: she had gone to see her boyfriend, not once, but twice.

We were made to understand soon after arrival that the Salvation Army considered our boyfriends stumbling blocks to our future restoration to the ranks of the virtuous. A Roman

Catholic might have said that for us, our boyfriends, the fathers of our babies, were to be considered the occasion of sin. Gloria's boyfriend was a high school dropout who was AWOL from the Army. He had gone into the armed forces without a real choice; he enlisted to avoid being beaten up or worse by Gloria's father and uncles. He probably located her with her help; surely Clare and Angela and I were not the only people who could operate a pay phone. They had called and even written for several weeks, which no one knew, until he convinced her to come to him. He went AWOL and, on the first free Wednesday afternoon that she could manage it, she joined him. The following morning when she told him she was going to return to Catherine Booth, he beat her up. She returned about lunchtime with two black eyes, and Brigadier Smith, the administrator, was more than prepared to do battle. Blood and fire!

Gloria was kept in a solitary room that most of us did not know about while her boyfriend was found and placed in confinement. Clare and Terry and I were horrified that when Gloria was released from isolation she was enraged to hear that her boyfriend was in custody of the military police. For she had gone over to the man's side; she was angry and bitter that her boyfriend was imprisoned, and she was furious about Brigadier Smith's part in it. She glared at the staff and spoke little to anyone.

A few days later she disappeared in the night and came back the following morning. Again she showed signs of having been beaten; a couple of ribs were broken. Again she was placed in the confinement room while the staff pondered what to do. I do not know if the military had released the boyfriend or if Gloria had gone somewhere else where she had been beaten up; I only knew what my father had told me once, long before. A man who hits a woman is trash, no man at all. I could not believe any woman would voluntarily go to a man who had hurt her. The whole thing was incomprehensible to me.

We did not see Gloria again until she came to pack up her possessions. She was sent somewhere else, but we were not told where. I only recall her messy red hair and the ravaged face that she turned to us as she went downstairs to leave. She said nothing, she only looked, as if to say—what? I don't know. Several of us were standing in the hall when she left. We couldn't believe she was leaving, and we did not say good-bye.

It seems to me now that those few months were crammed with events that had lasting meaning for my life. That may be an exaggeration, but I remember Elizabeth, one of the cooks, telling me before I left that things had changed a great deal during those months at Catherine Booth. It was part of how the world was changing shape in 1967, and I am pretty sure that Elizabeth thought change was not such a good thing.

One of these changes was the institution of a therapy program for those of us in residence. A doctoral candidate from the University of Cincinnati had been coming weekly to interview us for his research; based on those interviews, he suggested that a therapy group might be of benefit. The group was organized not long after I arrived and I asked to join it. I remember next to nothing of our sessions, but in my ninth month we got into a conversation about the problems of readjusting to the world after our time here—after we gave away our babies and went back to the places where we got pregnant. Clare and I said that we wished that some girl who was coming back for her six-week postpartum checkup could talk to us about adjustment "after." The therapist must have passed this on, because it later transpired that I was the first postpartum girl to have such a conversation with residents. Clare, in her turn, did the same. Whether the practice continued I don't know.

Another change was even more momentous. A pretty fifteen-year-old entered the home in her third or fourth month of pregnancy. Betsy was a charmer and everyone liked her. There had been a big turnover just recently in the residence, with Kate and Louisa and Dorothy all gone, and things were dull and depressing. Betsy bubbled; she laughed; she made us laugh. She was a favorite.

It used to be accepted that crushes or, as the English used to call them, "pashes," were typical in the life of same-sex institutions. They did not necessarily mean that one was homosexual. Jane Eyre's intense following during her time teaching at a boarding school is one example of how these things worked themselves out; the relationship between Charles and Sebastian in *Brideshead Revisited* is another. Today passionate same-sex friendships have become so controversial that we forget that they used to be thought of as part of growing up, not necessarily an indicator of sexual orientation. As it happened, Betsy became the object of several crushes, and Clare was one of the afflicted.

When Betsy went into premature labor and gave birth to a small, weak infant who died when only a couple of days old, Clare went to pieces. She had gone to take Betsy her tray one day for lunch and found her crying. Betsy had just been told that her baby had died. Clare did what she could to comfort her, stoically completed her workjob, and went to lunch. After lunch she asked me to go out and walk around the grounds with her, which we did, and then she broke down and told me about Betsy's baby. Now it was my turn: I did what I could to comfort Clare, which didn't feel like much.

The Berlin wall between the girls' side and hospital side was so strong and effective that at first Clare and I were the only ones who knew about Betsy's baby. The response in the group was overwhelming: Why weren't we told? The therapist, who was not formally on staff and had no hand in policy-making, said he would speak to someone. The following day at lunch, Captain Green formally announced the death of Betsy's baby. She talked about grief and how it was normal and healthy, and she recommended prayer as a help to comfort the sorrowing. We all cried a lot. It was, I was told, the first time any formal acknowledgment was made of the situation of any girl who had gone to hospital side. Later, when Lucy's baby also died, an announcement was made almost immediately. Betsy's room was flooded with cards, gifts, and flowers. Terry took the extraordinary step of calling her parents and asking them to send flowers; Angela took some candy out of her junk food cache and sent it over. The wall to the hospital side had not been dismantled, but it had certainly been broached.

Meanwhile, in the therapy group, we began, very shyly and vaguely, discussing crushes. I had one, too. Nurse Carter, one of the delivery room nurses, was the object of my affection. When I was on duty at lunch serving the vegetables, and she appeared, my heart fluttered. Once Clare and I ran into her at the local supermarket and we had a stammering conversation about cookies and classical music. Clare and I were buying some kind of junk food we should never have been eating and here was Nurse Carter, whom I loved. Trying to hide the junk food, blushing furiously, I babbled on like an idiot, telling her I liked Bach. When I returned for my postpartum visit months later and found that Nurse Carter wasn't on duty that day, I was miserable.

Not long after the death of Betsy's baby, I found myself in trouble. I had been at Catherine Booth for two months, the halfway mark of my likely stay, and I thought I could simply coast through the rest. The trouble had to do with my job. I liked working in the kitchen; Jenny, Elizabeth, and Mrs. Walker, the cooks, were among the first adult black women I ever knew outside of my high school French teacher, a slender New Orleans Creole who had lived for ten years in Paris. The cooks were as ill-assorted as any three people could be. Jenny, the presiding bishop of the kitchen, was small, wiry, and crotchety. In every possible area of human existence she knew what was right and what was wrong, and nobody had better question her. Only Captain Green could overrule her and get away with it. Elizabeth was taller, rounder, and grayer of hair than Jenny, although I suspect that she was ten years younger. Elizabeth reminded me of my father's mother who had died when I was fourteen, with the same gentle spirit and profound faith. She was also, in my view, a better cook than either of the other two and knew more about food than the dietician. I loved her, and I think she was fond of me.

Mrs. Walker, the third member of the triumvirate, immediately distinguished herself to a new kitchen worker by her use of her last name. She was younger than Jenny and Elizabeth and very assertive; she expected poor white trash like me, who had no morals and no sense and had let some man do what he wanted with her, to call her Mrs. Walker just as I would a school teacher or the preacher's wife. In the hierarchy of life, Mrs. Walker symbolically crushed us under her feet, and then made us some special treat to show she had a heart. She did make excellent fried chicken, better even than my mother's, and when I told her so she decided she liked me. Whenever I was down, I asked Mrs.

Walker to make us fried chicken and nearly every time she juggled the meal plan so she could.

I don't remember exactly what went wrong. All I know is that one day Mrs. Walker told me to do one thing and Jenny told me to do another, and I did what Mrs. Walker told me to do rather than what Jenny told me to do. Furthermore, I tried to defend my mistake. It was sheer stupidity on my part. I always could have gone back to Mrs. Walker and pleaded Jenny's tyranny. But for Jenny there was no higher authority. I had disobeyed and then "sassed." I was banished in tears, but what's worse, I was reported.

It was then I made the second of my two visits to Brigadier Smith's apartment. The first time I had gone was in my early days at Catherine Booth in order to get a needle for the sewing machine. Each girl who wanted to sew had her own personal needle; the needles were not left in the machines as one would do at home. So I went when I was told to go and knocked on the door. A short, chubby woman with gray hair wearing a nurse's uniform gestured me into a small, stuffy, overstuffed apartment. It was like stepping back in time: the dark Victorian furniture, the fussy doilies and fringed lampshades, and the clutter created an aura of claustrophobia, and yet it also felt home-like and safe. The Brigadier rummaged in a drawer and found me a needle and asked me a few questions about how I was getting along, and then offered me a cookie and sent me on my way. I left her apartment puzzled. She reminded me of no one so much as a friend of mine's Jewish grandmother. From her concern about whether I thought I was getting enough to eat to her accent to the dreidel I noticed in her drawer, she was more like a real Jewish grandmama than anything else I could think of.

On my second visit, she was like nobody's grandmama, Jewish or otherwise. She was in her Salvation Army uniform and she was in earnest. Standing erect, lacking nothing in moral certitude, she spoke to me at length about respecting my elders and being obedient to those whom God had set over me. I listened for a while and then cried, which seemed to amaze her. Incoherently I explained the conflict, as I understood it, in the kitchen. She listened and then offered me a cookie, although I was twenty pounds overweight and the doctors were furious with me. She told me again that I had to be obedient; I told her I would do anything to be reinstated in the kitchen. She said I would have to apologize to Jenny and then she dismissed me.

Unquestioning obedience? I'd never experienced anything like it. In high school I had been in a drum-and-baton marching group so I knew a little about military discipline, but this was unbelievable. I knew enough to know what Brigadier Smith's dismissal meant. I executed a crisp about-face and left the room. There was nothing more to be said.

Angry and aching, I went for a walk on the grounds and saw Nurse Carter. The home was a small community, and very little transpired, I had come to understand, that the staff did not know about. Nurse Carter saw me and my sore red eyes and took me in her arms. I cried more, and more completely, more cleansingly, than I ever could have done with Brigadier Smith, even in her Jewish grandmama mode, babbling angrily about how badly I was being treated and how it was not my fault, expecting somehow that Nurse Carter would side with me. Instead she held me at arm's length and said firmly that I must do as I was told, I must submit, I must apologize. I raged and she held me firmly; her face was sad, but she was not to be shaken. Time stood still while she held me and I composed myself; then she sent me with a kiss on the forehead to my room.

Before lunch the next day Captain Green led me into the kitchen where Jenny waited. I made my act of submission and was absolved. I went back to working and tried to walk carefully when Jenny was on duty. One Sunday evening when I was on duty with Mrs. Walker, she made a backhanded reference to my problem with Jenny. Clearly Mrs. Walker was impressed that I had taken her word over Jenny's. "Any time you want fried chicken, child, you just talk to Mrs. Walker," she said fiercely. It was the nearest thing to an admission of affection that anyone I knew ever got from her.

It was only years later, pondering this event which was so trivial in one way, that its full importance began to occur to me. I had grown up in what could be considered in every respect a typical white working-class family, with all the assumptions of such a background. My parents were more-or-less New Deal Democrats, my father an ardent union man. Yet they and I, our supposed liberalism notwithstanding, would never have imagined a situation where other whites would have required me, a white person, to submit to the authority of a black person, and certainly not a black kitchen worker. At Catherine Booth, there was no question about it. As a resident, the staff had authority over me. There was no wink of conspiracy or shrug of camaraderie from either Brigadier Smith or Nurse Carter to suggest that they "appreciated my problem." The rules and the expectations were the same for everyone; obedience was expected. It was too bad if Jenny was difficult but no one is perfect. And whatever was the case on the street outside the hospital, the rule inside was simple and applied to everyone. One was not meant to question the Pauline dictum, "Submit to those in authority over you." If I believed in racial equality as I claimed, I had to submit to Jenny's rule. I don't know if God was testing me in that, but it was one of the most difficult experiences of my life.

After I gave birth, a day before I was about to leave the hospital, Elizabeth came to my room. She brought me a bookmark with a Bible verse on it and told me to be a good girl. She confided that I was the first girl that Jenny had ever taken back after firing her, and I gave the credit for that to Captain Green. Elizabeth took my hand and prayed for me. The Bible says that the prayer of a good person availeth much, and in the dark and difficult years that followed my time at Catherine Booth, perhaps it was Elizabeth's prayers that upheld me.

FOUR

I went into labor on one of the last days of April, 1967, a good two weeks early. I had erratic but strong contractions all day and into the night. Nurse Carter stayed near me the whole time, but at midnight, after twelve hours of labor with only two centimeters of cervical dilation to show for it, she asked Dr. Jay to give me a shot of morphine to let me sleep. The morphine not only put me to sleep, it also stopped the labor. The following day I went back to the girls' side.

That was a Saturday and my parents or my grandparents were coming; I no longer remember which. They alternated weekends, and between us we had visited every small town in Kentucky and Southern Ohio that had a Howard Johnson or Big Boy restaurant. My grandparents bought me fabric and patterns so I could sew, usually accompanied by a double helping of the family gossip. I don't think that visiting me was as easy for my parents as it was for my grandparents—going to restaurants was not the high point of life for them as it was for my grandmother—and my mother and father grew more erratic and troubled the more pregnant I appeared. At one point my mother urged me to wear her wedding ring when we all went out together; I was appalled, and refused. But at least they came, which many of the other girls' families did not. Neither Clare nor Angela ever had a parent visit. Before my company arrived that Saturday, and after they dropped me off, Clare and I walked the corridors of Catherine Booth. Walking was supposed to be good for labor.

Halfway through chapel on Sunday morning my labor resumed with a vengeance. The first contraction tore through me like a tornado. I let out a groan, which was apparently strong enough to attract the attention of whichever nurse was on duty. She took me outside and we paced the halls for a while until my contractions grew more regular; then I went upstairs.

I had already been shaved on Friday when I was first admitted to hospital side; I had had one enema then, and now I had another. Blood and water poured from my vagina; I vomited; I screamed. Nurse Carter appeared like an angel and held my hand as labor intensified. Dr. Jay asked me if he could film the delivery, the most bizarre thing I had even heard of in my small-town Ohio life, but I scrawled a signature on the consent form. In the delivery room I struggled painfully to curl myself into a ball so that I could be given a spinal. Then my legs were spread and my ankles strapped to the stirrups, while my wrists were strapped to grips on the side of the delivery table. The spinal was quickly effective: there was no pain and no feeling in the lower part of my body. A tent-like drape was arranged over my legs. My son was born in the late afternoon of April 30, 1967.

"Look, look," said the delivery room nurse, and I watched him come out in the mirrors positioned at the foot of the delivery table. Everything was disconnected. It was as if it were not my body; it was as if he were not my child. That bloody, squalling mess was a child? They whisked him away. I waited for the episiotomy to be sewn up. Back in my room I asked for something to make me sleep, so I would not think about what had just happened. One of the disciplines to which I subjected myself after his birth was forgetfulness. Survival sometimes relies on such disciplines.

For twenty-four hours after the delivery I lay flat on my back to prevent spinal headache, and then waited another twenty-four to get out of bed because my episiotomy stitches still hurt. When

I first stood up, I felt like my entire internal organ system would fall out. The next day I had massive diarrhea from the chocolate-covered raisins that Clare had brought over, but finally I felt strong enough to do the one thing that I really wanted to do, which was to go and look at my son through the nursery window.

Nurse Carter came and walked with me at viewing time. The sweet-tempered black nursery nurse was on duty, and she cheerfully pointed out which baby was mine. He had fine black hair and was sleeping as if there was nothing in the world that could possibly harm him. I clung to Nurse Carter and looked at him, hearing in my mind the words from "Liverpool Lullabye," a Judy Collins song:

> Oh you have your father's face
> you're growing up a real hard case
> but there's no one who can take your place. . . .

That afternoon, he was taken to foster care.

When my mother arrived to take me home, she asked if I'd point the baby out to her. I told her he was gone, and she was deeply distraught. I had no idea she'd wanted to see the baby; the truth is, I'd been too self-absorbed to ask. Almost thirty years have passed, yet as I write this, the pain in remembering the first sight of my baby is as sharp as it was that day in 1967. But now, as then, I leave the room, close the door, and silence the grief. I say to myself, at least I did not kill him, and it is enough. It has to be.

In the car on the way home I told my mother I never wanted to discuss any of this again. She agreed to my request. Thus I cultivated a little more forgetfulness. Neither she nor my father ever raised the issue, except when we had to, like making my appointment to complete the surrender papers. And the forgetfulness was so complete that until a couple of years ago when I broached the subject with her, I had forgotten that it was my request that had kept her silent for so long.

The week I went home, the top song on the pop music charts was "Ticket to Ride" by the Beatles. Someone told me that it was about a pregnant woman, that a pregnant woman in England got a free train pass for British Rail. My English friends now tell me that isn't true, but that story was one of the sharp little barbs I chastised myself with, long ago.

I went back to my grandmother's, where I lived most of the summer while I worked at an insurance company. Perhaps Grandma sympathized more readily with my empty womb and empty arms because her own first son had died in early childhood. She cared for me lovingly, if distantly. My parents rarely came to see me and it took me years to understand that they were grieving too. I spent my evenings watching westerns on television with my grandfather.

To a certain degree I had gone into hiding again. All of my high school friends had disappeared, or so it seemed. My days came and went in the insurance office, and on the bus back and forth from the office. I struggled to lose the twenty extra pounds I'd brought home from the hospital. Clare came and spent the last week of August with me while I had two wisdom teeth removed. We tried to talk about what had happened that year, but we couldn't do more than stammer out a few words. How can you forget if you keep dragging up the past? I did find out, however, that Clare's doctor had given her birth control pills, saying that now that she had started having sex, she'd never be able to stop. That was a frightening idea. I had every intention of staying away from sex for the rest of my life, and I had written to my baby's father and told him I didn't want to see him anymore as a piece of that resolution. I wanted desperately to be back in the realm of ordinary life. In September I returned to college.

Once there I applied myself to my studies, since they at least seemed real; not much else did. Campus events embarrassed me, and except for depressing Chekhov plays and classical music concerts produced by the performing arts division, I attended nothing on campus. My friends had gone in other directions, quite literally, as the girls I knew were all dating or trying to date men from Wabash College. I spent my weekends in a half-empty dorm, and played loud rock music to silence my interior monologue. Somehow I could never work up the confidence to tell my story even to the woman from my college group to whom I was closest, while my two male friends, who had driven all the way to Dayton to visit me back in January, were distant as well. One was now involved with a girl I considered stupid, while the other was vague and reserved, always watching me with narrow eyes through the smoke of his endless cigarettes. I snubbed them both and was eventually able to join the ranks of those dating a Wabash man. Wabash, only an hour away from Indianapolis, was a useful escape, although at the football games and dances and beer parties I felt like I was standing outside myself watching myself trying to fit in.

I returned to ballet class, which, as a theater major, I could substitute for sports like volleyball and field hockey. In my advanced barre section, a new master was in charge. He was supposed to be from the Ballet Russe; as far as I was concerned he was straight from the Gulag. He proceeded down the barre the first day of class and slapped three-quarters of us on the belly with his riding crop. "Fat!" he would screech with each thwack. "Fat!" For me this was adding insult to injury—after all, that chubby tummy came from having a baby, a baby I had to stop thinking about, but how could I stop thinking about it if he kept reminding me?

The past was fleeing from me in every direction. My high school friends were rapidly growing into other lives that did not include me: Hannah was in Peru, and Jon was engaged to the girl he had started dating in our senior year of high school. My former roommate, Lina, had transferred to the University of Illinois and was living with a woman she was involved with. I knew very well that if I didn't make a point of trying to maintain human contact, I would wind up even more isolated and miserable. I made new friends—Eliza, a Southerner, who had an infectious laugh and kept me company on the long weekends when my friends were with their boyfriends, and Denise, who was an English major and considered "brainy." I enjoyed our intense conversations about William Blake and Emily Dickinson until I realized that she was courting me, but whether for her sorority or herself, I couldn't tell. I visited Clare, and we drove through the streets of Oxford, Ohio where she went to college, with her guitar and my autoharp, singing songs that we made up as we went along. She was well into the hippie scene, her blonde hair now waist-length and shining in the sun.

I suppose that my sense of disorientation and loss was partly because I had never been allowed to grieve the loss of my child. I knew he was not dead; at least I assumed not. He was alive enough for me to have to sign surrender papers, and you cannot give away what does not exist. But he was lost to me. My body had nourished him for nine months, I had watched his birth as well as I could, I had seen him. He was real, his feet and hands and the shape of his mouth indelibly imprinted on my memory. He was with me; then he wasn't. But in the secrecy and suppression that was normal for the world of Ohio of 1967, I went from one place where I was expected not to acknowledge my child's loss, to another. Even with Clare, ignoring things was the rule. She told me her mother had found her birth control pills, and then said, "Oh, well, I'm just an ostrich about these things." Just as when someone says to you, "Don't think about elephants!" and suddenly that is all you can think about, as soon as someone said, "Don't think about the baby," all I could think about was the baby. And I didn't want to tell anyone that I couldn't stop thinking about the baby, because I didn't want to hear yet another person say, as Clare had done, and as Lina had done, "You are going to drive yourself crazy if you don't stop this."

Second semester I moved into an oversized dorm room with four friends from my first year. I thought that with five of us living together my loneliness would be diminished. Instead it was worse, as we traveled to visit our various boyfriends while still trying to find time and space to study. Nights alone in the cavernous room, formerly a lecture hall, left me sleepless and scared. I switched from rock to Bach organ music.

One night, moved by a small hope of understanding, I told the man from Wabash College whom I was dating. I guess, at this point, it was not a big risk. He and I had talked at length about feeling like outsiders. He was majoring in biochemistry in order to please his parents, who wanted him to go to medical or dental school. I was suffering through an education minor to appease my parents, who wanted me to have "something to fall back on." He was reading theology and wanted to paint. I wanted to write, period. He was as much an oddity at Wabash as I was at Butler. I tend to think we fell in love commiserating.

So it happened that we began to talk about what we'd like to do with our lives other than what our parents wanted. He told me some rather nefarious things about his life, and I told him about my baby. Perhaps I was feeling reckless, or maybe I thought I could get rid of this man whom I actually liked and cared about by shocking him. Perhaps I could find consolation for my misery and loneliness. Incredibly, to me, he understood what I was going through; he was kind and compassionate and I could allow myself to cry a little. It was almost too much for me, and my gratitude was deep at finally finding someone with whom I could talk about the distress everyone else seemed to think I should be over by now. He seemed to need that connection as deeply as I did, and not long after that we began talking about getting married. In May we got engaged, and I joined two of my roommates in having our weddings in the summer of 1968. I quit school and moved to Wabash and worked in the college bookstore while my husband finished his senior year. He was offered a considerable scholarship to attend Harvard Divinity School, so in the heat and heaviness of the summer of 1969 we arrived in Cambridge, Massachusetts.

The streets of Cambridge that summer affected me as the streets of London must have affected Tom Jones or David Copperfield when they first arrived there. Above the infernal car-honkings, the leaden stink of the city buses, the constant harassment on the sidewalks by spare-changers and cult recruiters, and the dread mockery that Harvard silently made of all who were not of its caste, above all that was the sense of life being lived here in a fashion more intense, more important, and more self-aware than anywhere else I had been. Even my two adolescent forays to New York City to march with my drum-and-baton group in Macy's Thanksgiving Day parade had not affected me so strongly. In Cambridge I discovered chamber music through a neighbor who played the violin professionally, first encountered Jungianism through another neighbor who later became my therapist, and shopped at Filene's Basement. But more important than any of these, in Cambridge I encountered for the first time two very different institutions that would each transform my life.

. . . .

One was the Episcopal Church and the other was the women's liberation movement.

After I left Catherine Booth, my involvement with Christianity had been sporadic. In a way, that was the continuation of an older story. Fascinated even as a child by religion, I devoted my fourth-grade extracurricular reading to a series of books on religions other than Christianity. I may have been one of the rare kids who really loved Sunday school. My parents occasionally came to church on Christmas and Easter, but for the most part they felt, along with hundreds of thousands of American parents, that Sunday school might be necessary for children but a commitment to and experience of collective worship was of no real importance. Once when I queried my father, he told me he was a nondenominational Protestant but that he thought that most churches were congregations of hypocrites.

Glad Tidings Chapel, where I began my Sunday school career at the age of six, belonged to a peculiar nineteenth-century conservative American sect which took Paul's writing about Abraham in the fourth chapter of Romans as one of its central tenets. Its adherents opposed the Trinity as an invention of the Great Whore of Babylon, the Roman Catholic Church. They baptized by full immersion in the name of Jesus only and condemned anyone who did it any other way; they also condemned smoking, drinking liquor, dancing, card-playing, board games that used dice, and in general, movies, although *The Ten Commandments* was permitted. For all their severity, however, most of the people I met in that church were kind and relatively good examples of people who have found joy in knowing Christ. The mark against them for rabid anti-Catholicism was, strangely enough, balanced by their earnest repudiation of anti-Semitism. In Sunday school I was frequently told that the Jews were God's chosen people, that Jesus was a Jew, and that mistreatment of the Jews was a terrible sin. Unlike most conservative Christians, they apparently had no agenda for converting the Jews.

But when I was fourteen, I walked out of that little church forever. The reason was simple: I saw the pastor's wife severely beat one of her children, a girl of eight or nine. My father's words about hypocrites rang in my ears. When after several weeks' absence, my former Sunday school teacher came visiting to find out why I was not attending church, I told her. I also told her that I would not come back as long as that woman was in the church. There is no self-righteousness that quite compares to that of the morally indignant teenager.

I did not attend church with any regularity again until 1983, although while I was in high school I kept trying. Hannah, the friend whose letter would later make me think twice about an abortion, during our school years won all the prizes that her synagogue's Hebrew school could offer. I remember that she didn't eat pork or, in Passover, leavened bread. Once we went out after school, and she ordered a hamburger with no bun, pulled some matzoh out of her purse, and ate the hamburger (with some difficulty) on matzoh. She used to try to explain Judaism to me, and she could describe the history and practices of the Jews with the same humor and detail that she could talk about Byron and Shelley. Whether she actually believed in God was another matter: I think she did, but vaguely.

My best friend, Becky, had been raised an indifferent Protestant and actually believed in God and Jesus, but wasn't altogether certain why it mattered. When we were juniors in high school, she began dating the son of a local Evangelical United Brethren pastor, and so we went to church at her boyfriend's father's church. Ironically, it was same church where I had been baptized as a two-year-old. I startled the high school Sunday school teacher with my knowledge of the Bible, but I was doing it with a "froward spirit" and putting him on the spot with proof-texts from Scripture. After I stopped attending church, my teacher sent me this verse from the King James Bible: "They that are of a froward heart are an abomination to the Lord, but such as are upright in their ways are his delight" (Prov. 11:20). A more modern version translates "froward heart" as "crooked mind."

Once I could drive, I didn't have to tag along with anyone and could go church shopping every few weeks, even sampling the Reform and Conservative synagogues. At college, I often attended the Saturday late-afternoon Mass at the Catholic church nearby. My Roman Catholic grandmother, my father's mother, was long since dead, but I never forgot the lyric beauty of the sung Mass of her funeral. I loved the liturgy of the Catholic Church, even if I was uncertain about its theology. Sometimes I walked over with a Catholic boy I'd made friends with, sometimes with one of the Catholic girls from my dorm. It may well be that an anti-abortion sermon given in that church influenced my decision not to have an abortion that year, but I can no longer remember whether I heard that sermon in the fall of 1966 or the following year, when I had returned to my college and was still occasionally attending Mass and trying to make sense of it all.

My formal introduction to the Episcopal Church occurred one day in early winter when my husband's former Wabash room-mate arrived in Cambridge for a visit and urged us to come to church with him. My husband was in seminary, after all, with some vague notion of being ordained—he was never very clear about it—and his ex-roommate took us to the Church of the Advent on Beacon Hill. Even the Roman Catholic ceremonies I had attended, one of which was my grandmother's funeral Mass sung by the teaching brothers of her parish church's school, could not compare to the Church of the Advent on its feast day, the first Sunday in Advent. Isabel Stewart Gardiner's twenty-three-karat gold cross led the procession, accompanied by enough incense to sweeten all of Beacon Hill—and I had thought dinner at the Hare Krishna house in Brookline was heavy on the smells.

Strangely enough, I had already discovered the Episcopal Church, although I didn't know it yet. Down on Memorial Drive in Cambridge I had found the chapel of a monastery one hot evening when my husband was working and I was walking alone. I went inside the cool, faintly glowing chapel and sat, as I often did when I had found a Catholic church and there was no one I knew around to notice me going in. Eventually the brothers entered and had some kind of a service—I seem to recall chant-ing—and I sat in the back and listened, scarcely knowing what I was hearing. Some evenings, unknown to anyone, including my husband, I wandered over there to listen and to try to pray. Pray to whom? Pray for what? I couldn't say. Once I said, "Anybody home?" into the darkness, and waited, half-defiant, half-amused at myself, for an answer.

. . . .

There were midnight masses on Saturday nights at the Episcopal church in Harvard Square; someone invited me, I no longer recall who. Twenty or so people sat on the floor and passed around a jug of Chianti and homemade bread for communion while we talked about God and the war in Vietnam. I went twice, maybe three times. But who was this God they talked about? The exacting rulemaker from my childhood and from Hannah's brand of Judaism? The benign uncle of some of the churches I visited in high school? Captain Green's strict but forgiving commander-in-chief? The distant, glorious, unapproachable king of the Church of the Advent? Or the wine-swilling, pacifist buddy of the priest who supervised the Harvard Square midnight masses? The cults and the street scene were easier to understand, easier to enter into. Except for my solitary visits to the monastery chapel, I abandoned Christianity that year.

One day the following spring, before my husband and I moved back to Indiana, I walked up and down the banks of the Charles River. The sailboats were out, slipping merrily along the glistening water. Yet as I watched them, I could only think of mayflies, which flare and flutter their white wings for one day of life before they die. On that most beautiful day, having just learned that I was pregnant again, I did not rejoice in the newness of life but turned melancholy. I thought of how short and sad life is, how we flutter and glisten for a day and then are nothing. Walking back toward Harvard Square, I noticed the monastery chapel and slipped in. In the soft gray-gold light, I asked a God I no longer understood or perhaps even believed in to save and protect this new life in me. This one would be mine; this one nobody would be allowed to take away. Fourteen years later I brought my daughter, Shannon, back to that chapel on Memorial Drive, but I could not explain to her why taking her there mattered so much to me, or why I dragged her out of bed to come a distance across Boston to spend Sunday morning in that elegant small sacred space. Things like gratitude and holy ground are hard to explain, and anyway, they are best discovered for oneself.

FIVE

It seems that there are moments in everyone's life where God shows his hand, where he says in effect, Here I am. My Presbyterian friend tells me that to be able to recognize and appreciate such moments is the result of prevenient grace, the work of God in our lives even when we don't know him, to prepare us for his coming. God had been working on me for a long time before the day I am about to describe, but I just couldn't see it. My mother used to tell a joke about a farmer whacking his mule in the head with a board. A city slicker complained that the farmer was hurting the mule. The farmer replied that he was only trying to get the mule's attention. This is how God finally got my attention.

When the eighties began, I was well over thirty and felt I had become a grown-up at last. Reluctantly I had ended my marriage to my daughter Shannon's father and was living in Amherst, Massachusetts when, in 1978, I remarried. Our son, Geoffrey, was born a year later to the day. In 1982 Bill and I realized that we had been in Amherst for ten years and it dawned on us that we were done with that place. So when Bill was offered a teaching position at Sarah Lawrence College in Bronxville, New York, we packed up the kids and the dogs and our record collection and moved. Someone had once said I was the sort of person who would never leave a town like Amherst, and I was glad at least to have proved that wrong.

The January after our move, when Shannon had just turned twelve and Geoff was three, the children and I set out to drive to Massachusetts for a long weekend. The day began blue and brilliant and then, suddenly, demonically, the road led us into an unexpected blizzard. I found myself driving first in limited and then zero visibility, and the car's traction disappeared as well. Then it began: the spinning. The car began to wheel wildly around, circling, bouncing off the guard rails, circling again. Finally we came to a jolting stop against the center rail. Fearful that the car might catch on fire, I shrieked to the children to get out. Geoff was still in his car seat, and Shannon and I fumbled with it to free him. We stood on the narrow snow-covered strip in the center of the parkway shivering. Now what?

The car did not explode; it sat looking sad and smashed. The kids began to complain about the cold, and I thought perhaps we could get back in the car. But what if we were in the car and someone ran into us? Or what if someone ran into us as we stood in the middle of the road? For the third time in five minutes I turned my thoughts to God. I had cried out to him first when the car began spinning; again when I struggled to get Geoff out of the car seat; and now again, not knowing what to do. Help me, oh help me, not for me but for the children.

For a third of my life I had thought I was working my way free from the religion of my childhood. And for a third of my life I had been secretly longing for God to prove me wrong. Maybe I wanted a "road to Damascus" experience. Maybe that's what I got.

Two flashing yellow lights appeared through the white nightmare. A pickup truck with two huge strobe lights mounted on the roof came to a stop behind my car. A man leapt out and ran to us. "Are you okay?" He examined my car, got in it, and turned on the engine. It started. He got a crowbar from his truck and pulled the bent fender away from the front left tire. "Follow me," he said. He drove slowly down the road to the nearest exit and guided us off to a gas station. A man there looked over the car and glanced at me and my children and shook his head.

Before the man in the pickup left us, he told me, "God is taking care of you. Don't worry." For years I thought he was an angel; I still do, but now I know that God sends angels in human as well as heavenly form. In this case, the human form was the representative of a utility company called United Illuminating. I discovered about two years ago that the logo UI on his truck stood for that Connecticut utility. I liked the idea. Not only did his truck illuminate our escape from the blizzard-blind road, his words and his kindness illuminated my spirit in the cruel whiteness of that disastrous day.

When the storm cleared I managed to drag our battered car home. The day that had started off in happy anticipation ended with us all scared and sad. Geoff didn't sleep well that night, and neither did I. All of us suffered from minor forms of whiplash, with aching necks and backs. I was sleepless for several nights, and my anxiety didn't lessen when insurance adjustors looking at the car tactlessly expressed surprise that none of us had been injured. We later heard that they had been surprised that none of us were killed. Furthermore, that nearly-destroyed car had brought us home—and then stopped running.

A few weeks after the accident I bought a New English Bible from a thrift shop bin for fifty cents and began reading it every day. It had notes, unlike my old King James Bible, and I liked the notes. They gave me an idea of what was going on and I hungered to know.

As I've said, I have always had plenty of contact with religion. My father's mostly Catholic family cheerfully broke the bourgeois rule that proper people don't discuss religion or politics: they argued about both at every opportunity. After I finished reading through my elementary school library series on the major world religions, I studied Buddhism, especially Zen. As a hippie in Cambridge I investigated the Hare Krishnas and Transcendental Meditation, and chanted all night with Baba Ram Dass. While finishing my undergraduate degree in Amherst, I began seeing a Jungian therapist, a project that represented, for me at least, an important effort to shed the Christianity of my youth and escape the hound of heaven for what seemed more congenial—the Great Mother, the Goddess. My Jungian therapist seemed to assume that my parents were pressuring me in some way regarding Christianity, in spite of the fact that religion was the last thing they were worried about; my sojourn in a commune and my divorce from Shannon's father had nearly driven them to distraction.

Like so many people who think of themselves as "spiritual," I was unable or unwilling to acknowledge the possibility of a supernatural power far stranger, far more profound, and far more complex. None of the popular substitutes for Christianity made much in the way of an ethical claim on the lives of those who followed them, and that was part of their appeal.

The writer of the letter to the Hebrews says it is a terrible thing to fall into the hands of the living God; I once heard Terry Fulham respond that it is a more terrible thing to fall out of the hands of the living God. By the time Bill's and my son was born, I figured I was well out of those hands. That was just about when the sense of strangeness set in. The first time it showed itself was when I asked my husband about the topic of his doctoral dissertation and he told me he was going to write about the theology of the poet John Milton. When he began reading Reformation theology, I asked him, in some amazement, whether he believed in God. He hesitated for a minute and then said, "I'm willing to accept him as a metaphor." What on earth did that mean?

One night I was watching television, the serialization of Evelyn Waugh's novel *Brideshead Revisited*. It was the episode where old Lord Marchmain is dying. A lapsed Catholic who had left his humorless, devout wife to live in Venice with his considerably livelier mistress, he has returned to his ancestral home to die. As death is imminent, his mistress and daughter call a priest to administer the last rites. Astonishingly, at the conclusion of the rite, the comatose Lord Marchmain makes the sign of the cross. At that I burst into tears. Sobbing, I telephoned a friend of mine and said I was going to end up a Roman Catholic.

At the time I assumed I was simply getting strange, but I also had a nagging sense that the strangeness I was experiencing had something to do with this God I worried about so much. What else but strangeness would have led me to spend a day searching out a passage from an antiquated book called the Bible that I didn't even believe in any more? What else but strangeness would have made me shed tears when old Lord Marchmain made the sign of the cross on his deathbed, or led me to sneak into churches that I happened to find open and sit there for an hour gazing at a cross or an altar or a stained glass window, longing for the emptiness in my heart to be filled?

On an ordinary Sunday in August of 1983 I found myself sitting in an ordinary Episcopal church because a friend was in town and had invited me to go to church with him. Since then I have learned that more commitments to Christ come from that basic act of simple asking than from any dramatic and unexpected conversion experience. So it was with me. It was summer, but not horribly so. My friend, a longtime Episcopalian, was coming for a weekend, and asked me to check in advance if there was an Episcopal church in town for him. As it happened, the girl who babysat for me was the daughter of the local rector, so I called and asked her about services. Easy as that. On Sunday morning my friend casually asked if anyone cared to join him, and I nervously asked if he minded if I went along. I wanted to examine the babysitter's father, whom I had seen once before weeding his garden in Union Jack swimming trunks—not exactly my recollection of clerical behavior from my youth.

That church was and is a magnificent example of the Gothic revival. The mass of its gray stone edifice belies the delicacy of the interior. A spectacular stained glass window above the altar depicts Christ blessing the children. I stood gazing at some of the most glorious stained glass windows I had ever seen in my years of surreptitious church visits. Meanwhile, my babysitter's father was nowhere to be seen. As my friend looked into the sheaf of papers that had been thrust into our hands at the door, he groaned. "Terrible lessons," he said. "I don't know what she'll do with them."

"*She?*" I asked blankly.

"She. The priest. Here's her name." He pointed to the leaflet.

"Women can't be priests," I insisted.

"Yes, they can," he smiled. Thrusting the hymnal at me for the processional, he added, "Some feminist you are."

The sermon affected me strongly. When I asked the priest—who was the parish associate—for a copy of it a few years later, she was embarrassed and said it wasn't really very good. When I reread it, I saw she wasn't just being modest, but it didn't matter. She preached what I needed to hear, which was God's untiring love for the creatures made in his image. For in her words I understood at last what the heart of my strangeness was, and it was my need for that love. After the service was over, my friend and I walked to a small park near the town tennis courts and he told me about his own faith. I asked him, plaintively, "Now what am I going to do?" He was the same friend I had phoned two years earlier, sobbing at the end of *Brideshead Revisited*; now we laughed. One or the other of us said, if not on that occasion then another, God can even work through television.

I still did not connect this church with the spectacular event on Beacon Hill a dozen years earlier, nor with the cool, glowing monastery chapel that had been my refuge in Cambridge. I had no sense of the Episcopal Church, the Anglican Communion, the Thirty-nine Articles, or the Anglican "three-legged stool" of scripture, reason, and tradition. I just knew that this was the place where God and I had found common ground, and I had to come back. Later in the fall my babysitter's father returned from vacation and finally stepped into the pulpit, and I began to be instructed in an ideal of Christianity that sounded like nothing I had ever heard before. He spoke of the sacraments, and God's real presence in them. God, it seemed, was not a something out there, but a someone in here, in this water, in this bread, in this wine, acting to make us new. He spoke of the Anglican conception of the delicate balance of freedom and authority, and how God's respect for our freedom is so great that he even allowed his own Son to be killed rather than violate the freedom of the human being made in his image. He spoke of human social responsibility, and I learned later that he and this congregation had fought first to house Vietnamese boat people and later mentally handicapped people in an apartment in the parish house, thus earning the wrath of their upper-middle-class neighbors. I liked the idea of a church that cared for the disadvantaged. I was told there had been some defections from the church during the Vietnam War era when the rector stopped using "Onward Christian Soldiers" at the request of a couple whose son had died in Vietnam.

Including a woman priest on the staff smashed all my carefully cultivated feminist objections to Christianity. Male priests serving a male God? I guessed that was at least half wrong. If this was a church that took women seriously enough to make them ministers (the word I would have used then), then maybe it was the place for me. I liked her very much: she was warm and funny, and she talked to me about Jesus without the cloying sentimentality of my childhood church. She understood my years of wrestling with God and seemed to think such behavior was fairly common—that I was not a terrible person. Early on I told her about my divorce and the baby I had given up for adoption. Maybe in that she was not as penetrating as she might have been, but she reassured me that God didn't hate me and that God had forgiven me. Maybe she heard within my fretting and questioning how deeply I needed to forgive myself. So many Sundays I would stand and stare at the stained glass window of Mary, vibrantly rich in red and blue hues, above the choirloft in my parish church. First I would make myself remember that she, too, had a child in scandalous circumstances. And then I would think, "My parish. My church. My home." It only took a few weeks for me to begin to say it.

I needed my baptismal certificate so I could be admitted to Holy Communion. How I longed for that now! I had been baptized, so my mother had told me. Actually I'd been baptized twice, or possibly three times—first as a small child in the Evangelical United Brethren Church and then as an eleven year old in my odd little church that did not believe in infant baptism. Not long after that baptism, my father's mother informed me that neither one of those counted, since she had arranged for her parish priest to come over and baptize me one day when I was a few weeks old and my parents weren't around. But I had no proof of any of them. My mother finally found the certificate, but before she sent it she called me and asked grimly, "What happened?" as if only some monstrous trauma like rape or near murder could have led to such a dramatic change.

The sense of fitness and truth and reality that Christianity allowed to me was, and remains, almost inexplicable. Daily I hear things and see things and find myself saying, "Yes, so that's how it is." Recently I was introduced to G. K. Chesterton's *Orthodoxy* by my son's guitar teacher. In chapter three, "The Ethics of Elfland," Chesterton describes the origins of his Christian faith in childhood experience. Among them he mentions fairy tales, with their strict moral precision, and the implacable sense of "fairness" that all small children have, and his sense of the strangeness and preciousness of the cosmos. All these guided him, albeit unconsciously, to the Christian faith. When I read this I had an extraordinary sense of déjà vu: everything I felt so strongly for so many years had been a signpost to Christianity, but I could not know that until I had finally crossed over the border and given my allegiance to a new kingdom.

The strangeness didn't stop there. A few months after I returned to the church, around Christmas, while out shopping I passed the Salvation Army man ringing his bell beside the red kettle. I stood and watched, feeling an ache so deep I trembled. For fifteen years I had turned my head every time I passed one of them; I didn't want to see and I didn't want to remember what the sight of him might make me remember. I had wanted to hate them, and tried to think of them as my oppressors, but I had been lying to myself all along. A gate swung open within me. 1967 and everything that happened then stood before me, longing to be freed.

I fumbled in my purse and threw the biggest bill I had into the Salvation Army bucket. The man looked amazed. "Thank you!" I couldn't reply, but ran to my car and curled up behind the steering wheel while I wept. Where was my baby? Was he all right? Would I ever see him again?

"You can't ask those questions," I told myself. "Shut up. Wipe off the tears, go home and make dinner."

Then another voice said, "You don't have to live that way any more. Don't be afraid. He's all right. And you're forgiven."

I wanted to believe the second voice, but it took a while.

SIX

Thanksgiving, 1987. Twenty-one years before I had been a pregnant teenager telling my parents the bad news. Now I was in my second year at the General Theological Seminary, an Episcopal seminary in New York City. Although I had no prospects of being ordained to the priesthood any time soon, I was determined to study theology and the Bible in order to present myself as a laborer who does not need to be ashamed and correctly handles the word of truth. There were practical reasons, too, because my children were asking me hard questions about Christianity—Shannon in particular, who was twelve when Bill and I reentered the church—and they were both too intelligent to settle for simple answers.

My children weren't the only ones with questions. I wondered what the real arguments were on both sides of the ordination of women, and how that related to the Bible and to nineteenth-century abolitionists I had heard of who encouraged women preaching—and what all of that might have to do with my own growing sense that I had some kind of calling to ministry. My seminary tutor had given me a biography of Mother Teresa as an aid to my efforts in discernment. He hoped that the story of Mother Teresa's own discernment process as God called her to found the Missionaries of Charity would help me focus. It did, but it also inspired me to arrange to spend January in Calcutta working with the Missionaries of Charity.

That November I had finals approaching, vaccinations to endure, and Christmas just around the corner. Relaxing with friends in their house in western Massachusetts would have been a perfect holiday, except for one thing. My period was late.

I was thirty-nine years old. I knew the risks of late childbearing, not only to the mother but to the child. At my age, the likelihood that the child would be damaged in some way was far greater than when I was pregnant with Geoff nine years earlier. Furthermore, this would be not only a problem pregnancy, it would be a disastrous pregnancy. The anti-malaria medication I would have to take in India can be notoriously toxic to the unborn child. I would have to choose among risking malaria, risking the child's health, or staying home, although the trip was something I wanted desperately to do. Nor did I see how, as a commuter student, I could finish seminary in three years with an infant in tow. True, I had always wanted another child, but that desire I had put aside some years earlier as period after period passed by. Now I was too old, I was getting on with my life, I had given away all the baby clothes.

Bill was as torn as I. He was in the middle of his tenure decision and might be looking for work the next year. If he didn't get tenure, we still planned to stay in our house and scrape by so that Shannon could finish high school in the place she had been for the past five years, but the prospect of a third child made scraping by feel a lot less plausible. He had ideas for research he wanted to do and new courses he wanted to develop; we both knew that if there was another child, he would want to be as involved in its care as he had been with Shannon and Geoff. His professional life, just getting off the ground, would be stalled.

When we got back from Massachusetts Bill and I bought a home pregnancy test kit. It took only a few minutes to see that the test was positive.

I went to the doctor, where the results of the pregnancy test were confirmed. I was about ten weeks pregnant. I must have looked so chagrined that the nurse asked brightly, "Is this a problem pregnancy?" Or perhaps it was just a routine question. How could she be so cheerful? I didn't want to answer her because I didn't want to have the conversation that must necessarily follow.

Finally I blurted out, "I'm not thrilled to be pregnant, but I think abortion is wrong, so that's not something I want to talk about." At this point in my conversion to Christianity I had become vaguely aware that I could never have an abortion, but in shutting off the conversation I was speaking to myself as much as to the nurse. Something was telling me (my gut? the Holy Spirit?) that aborting this pregnancy was wrong, but if someone had asked me to explain myself, I couldn't have.

"Oh!" the nurse said, still smiling broadly. "Well, go ahead and undress. Doctor will be back in a minute."

If I wasn't going to have an abortion, the HMO staff had nothing more to say to me. No offer of a counselor, no reference to a social worker to talk about food stamps or child care or any of the things that an unexpectedly pregnant woman might need. I didn't need food stamps or child care, but the nurse did not know that. She only knew one thing, which was how to line me up for an abortion—and this at one of the largest and best-known HMO's in the country. The doctor did his exam nonchalantly and had nothing much to add. I went home angry, frightened, miserable.

For the next few days Bill and I prayed hard, pleading with God to give us peace about this unexpected baby. We were both fractious, and I grew even more temperamental as my nausea grew. We realized we had to tell our children, and even that was painful and confusing. When I told Shannon and Geoff there was a baby on the way, their responses astonished me. Shannon, whom I thought would be embarrassed at her elderly mother getting pregnant, was delighted; Geoff, who had pestered us for years about a baby brother, burst into tears and ran from the dinner table. Most days I felt as though I was being tossed in a blanket.

A voice pestered me in my head when I could not sleep, or when I was stuck in traffic on the way to the seminary. The voice said: It's not that far along. You could have an abortion and tell Bill and the kids you miscarrried. How would they know the difference? Who would care but you? And once you get back from India you could go to confession and have it done with. It's no big deal. Everyone does it....

I fought to get the voice out of my head, to leave me alone. Every time I heard the voice I responded with the Jesus Prayer. Here I was a seminarian, maybe even someone who'd be ordained someday, and I had no better prayer to turn to than the one that had held me up when I was a barely believing teenager. I turned to the Rosary, hoping that Mary, who knew what it was like to be pregnant when you least expected it, would help me. Finally I began to feel some peace. One night after dinner, Bill and I sat down and talked for a long time. Finally it was all right. We could live with this. We relaxed and began thinking about names.

Our happiness lasted only a few days. One Monday morning I began to bleed, and by late afternoon I had miscarried. Our baby slipped out of my body as I lay on the bathroom floor, my knees pulled to my chest in agony. The amniotic sac was whole, and inside we saw the pale form of a tiny person. When we took the sac to the doctor (as we'd been instructed to do), he placed it in a glass jar containing a clear fluid and the dullness of the sac cleared. Suddenly the tiny form was visible in every detail: fingers and toes were separate and distinct; tissues that were becoming ears and eyes stood out in their specificity; the ridges of the vertebrae rose under the flesh of the back in perfect orderliness. The pain of what I was seeing was so great I could barely breathe.

The doctor sympathized with us over our loss, and offered to leave us alone for a while. We sent him away and clung to each other and mourned. A few days later, one of our priests read the burial office with us. When we had committed our child to his creator, we put our grief aside and tried to get on with our lives. Two weeks later, I boarded the Lufthansa jet that took me to New Delhi.

ᘐ

When I became an Episcopalian, changing my views on abortion was the furthest thing from my mind. Indeed, the preaching and teaching that I received in my parish church suggested that legal abortion was consistent with the Anglican conception of freedom. According to my rector, freedom was essential to Anglican Christianity and the whole point of the English Reformation was to allow God-given human reason the liberty it required to guide people into the right paths. Legalisms like those of Rome thwarted the flowering of reason and kept Christians from being able to face the new challenges of each generation.

In the case of abortion, Anglicanism had made a remarkable turnabout in a very short time. In 1958, the Lambeth meeting of Anglican bishops from throughout the world condemned abortion except to save the life of the mother:

> Christians reject the practice of induced abortion, or infanticide, which involves the killing of a life already conceived (as well as a violation of the personality of the mother) save at the dictate of strict and undeniable medical necessity.[2]

In 1967, the Archbishop of Canterbury, Michael Ramsey, argued on behalf of legalizing abortion in cases of risk to the physical or mental health of the mother, rape or incest, potential physical or mental abnormality on the part of the child, or "if bearing a child would prove beyond the mother's capacity."[3] Ramsey's remarks came at a time when a liberalized abortion bill had passed a second reading in the House of Commons. After *Roe v. Wade* was read into law by the United States Supreme Court in 1973, the Episcopal Church joined the American Baptist Church, the American Friends Service committee, the American Jewish Conference, the Disciples of Christ, and the YWCA in supporting the new legal status of abortion.[4] Its current position affirms the sacredness of human life and asserts the "tragic dimension" of abortion, but opposes anti-abortion legislation and urges that Episcopalians respect the conscience of the individual.[5] This was presented to me as evidence of the progressive mentality of Anglicanism.

Ironically, I had found a church that seemed to endorse most of my feminist theories at the same time that my returning memories of the baby I could not bring myself to abort unsettled years of feminist certainty. So I busied myself with the altar guild and Lenten Bible studies on Matthew (one year) and Revelation (the next) and said to myself that it was just my troubled history that made me uneasy.

Yet nothing was more shattering to my state of mind than an essay I came across by Stephen Jay Gould, the Harvard biologist, called "Human Babies as Embryos," in his book *Ever Since Darwin*. The strange title barely touches the essay's thrust: compared to other animals, the human infant comes into the world in a state of premature development. Newborn chickens and turtles scurry off in search of food soon after birth, and sophisticated measures of brain and bone and muscle place the human newborn in a lower stage of maturity than our primate cousins. What is thought of as birth-level development in the human newborn is fetal level in apes and monkeys.

As his essay sank in, the thought that entered my mind was, "Well, that shoots the viability argument out of the water." One consistent argument on behalf of legal abortion is that it is permissible to abort a fetus that is "non-viable"—that cannot survive on its own outside its mother. In the light of Gould's description of human development, however, that argument suddenly becomes unintelligible, since no human newborn survives outside the mother's body unassisted; indeed, few children under the age of six could. I tried to imagine Shannon or Geoff at the age of five fending for themselves, recalling François Truffault's film, *The Wild Child*. A child left alone dies or, as in the few documented cases of feral children, becomes a creature shut off from the rest of its human cousins. Whether in the womb or held in the arms, a child is dependent. How can one decide, then, at what point a human being achieves the level of self-sufficiency that the viability argument assumes without coming to approve of infanticide? Where do you draw the line?

I carried this thought around for months as I found myself irresistibly drawn to any article, book, or essay on abortion. I had been a supporter of the *Roe v. Wade* decision since it was first passed. My pro-abortion position, as I saw it, was a part of my adulthood, something I had lived with all my life. But Gould's essay upset my balance. I began looking more carefully at the rhetoric of abortion and undertook yet once more an examination of my own experience. Painfully, I forced myself to bring back memories I had struggled to keep out of sight, out of mind: my son, surrendered for adoption twenty years earlier; my parents, sympathetic but ashamed; and Catherine Booth, with its secure and supportive Christian environment. It seemed in 1967 that I had to make a virtue of forgetting, but suppressed shame and grief combined to make a hidden sore that I had carried silently and shared with almost no one. My old friend Clare had disappeared into Mexico several years earlier. I heard some time later from a mutual friend that she had become a Christian, but I had no contact with her, and after her disappearance, my isolation became complete. I had told Shannon's father about my lost child, and Bill, but it never quite worked out that sharing the sorrow divided it. Every time I confided in someone, I experienced the grief and loneliness more acutely. Shannon's father used to say that there was always around me "an aura of sadness."

Supporting legalized abortion was the way I dealt with a grief that nothing ever seemed to ease or assuage. I had even written an article for an early feminist journal about giving up my baby, concluding rather incoherently that losing a living child had made me miserable but aborting that same child would have allowed me to be happy. I thought that if I had never felt him move, never seen his face, never had to think of him in some other woman's arms, somehow the agony of losing him would have been less acute, or would never have existed.

Further along in my reflections, a certain conversation began to haunt me. I remembered the group of women who were affiliated with the women's center where I worked when I went back to college. I had met a lot of feminists when I lived in Cambridge, from Trotskyite functionaries to Ayn Rand libertarians to the anarchists of Cell 16, and they had decisively altered my worldview. Whatever else these women disagreed on, they agreed with Engels that the subjection of women was the model for the subjection of nations and races under capitalism and imperialism. To liberate all humanity, begin with liberating women. I went to work at the women's center at the University of Massachusetts to further what I then saw as revolution. But it was not as simple as I thought it would be, because along with the counselors, lesbian activists, graduate students, and ex-hippies, there was a group of poor women, mostly on welfare, who were eventually driven out of the center because they disliked our abortion counseling and advocacy.

In the arrogant jargon of our politics, we had invited this group of women to the center to show our "solidarity" with them. We wanted to "celebrate their struggle." Some of the poor women were Marxists, some were Catholics, and some were neither, but they were almost all opposed to abortion. A war went on for months while they argued that the women's center should stop making abortion referrals. I was particularly troubled by the memory of a woman who waved the brochure we used to hand out from the local abortion clinic, which cited figures on how much cheaper it was to abort the children of the poor rather than provide for their health and welfare. "This is what you really think of us!" she cried. Another woman, a Puerto Rican, talked about forced sterilization and the development of what would become Norplant in her homeland. She used the word "genocide." I didn't understand because I didn't want to. The young feminists and older activists at the women's center all agreed that life was about getting jobs and having lovers and not being burdened by children. After all, that is what we thought men's lives were like and if we were to have equality with men, that is how we had to be.

But the poor women saw things differently. Although they were as ideologically assorted as any group of women could be, they shared the view that children were the future. To abort a child was to destroy a little bit of the future. One woman had a plaque on her desk that said, "A baby is God's opinion that the world should go on," while to the rest of the women at the center, God was something men invented to keep women from having any rights. Obviously there wasn't much room for conversation between the two groups. It occurs to me, all these years later, that the same disagreement about babies, freedom, and "rights" still exists between those who support abortion rights and those who do not.

The more I read and learned about abortion, the more I became convinced that the movement for abortion on demand had begun not in regard to the rights of women but the rights of men—or rather, some men. Historically, the first efforts at legalizing abortion originated with men, not women. Susan B. Anthony and other early feminists hated abortion, and saw it as a direct consequence of women's disenfranchisement. In 1869 Anthony wrote in the suffragist newspaper, *The Revolution*, "No matter what the motive, love of ease, or a desire to save from suffering the unborn innocent, the woman is awfully guilty who commits the deed...but oh! thrice guilty is he who drove her to the desperation which impelled her to commit the crime." Another early feminist, Mattie Brinkerhoff, went further: "When a man steals to justify hunger, we may conclude there is something wrong in society, so when a woman destroys the life of her unborn child, it is evidence that...she has been greatly wronged." Elizabeth Cady Stanton and Victoria Woodhull expressed similar views.[6]

I began pestering my rector about these questions, and he reiterated his view that freedom was a principal Anglican virtue and people had to be able to make up their own minds about things. His position sounded reasonable enough, but I always walked away troubled. What if freedom meant giving people enough rope to hang themselves? And what was the church going to do in a practical way to help people sustain problematic pregnancies in the face of abortion on demand? Did we have a better choice to offer? I believe he thought my persistent questioning would be aided by studying the issue further for myself, so he had me appointed to a diocesan ad hoc committee that was preparing a document for the 1988 General Convention to inform its deliberations on the question of abortion. He read me correctly on that account: that experience of study and debate was exactly what I needed.

For my work on that committee I read documents scientific, moral, feminist, Roman Catholic, and everything else, and drew some unpleasant conclusions. Pregnancy, it seems, is inconvenient to the functioning of modern postindustrial societies. Utilitarianism, that terrible gift of early nineteenth-century Britain, posits usefulness and efficiency as the moral indicators of worth. The English Utilitarians were the grandfathers of "the bottom line," and as human life moved through the centuries, the definition expanded of which members of society constitute a liability: poor women and children, the sick, the retarded, the unproductive. In Russia, Lenin legalized abortion early on; at that time no other birth control was available.[7] In 1962 the American Law Institute began to make the case for a liberalized—but not "on demand"—abortion law, with which the American Bar Association and the American Medical Association agreed in 1967. The ACLU began promoting completely legalized abortion in 1968, and the AMA got on board in 1970. By construing abortion solely as a medical procedure, the medical profession maintained control not only over its practice but also contributed to the bias that objectors to abortion were "unscientific" and "anti-health."[8]

I found that after the statements from Lambeth in the fifties, furthermore, Anglicans had no definitive writings to guide their deliberations and seemed to have little to say. I was one of two people out of twelve on the diocesan committee who were even slightly pro-life. At the end of our sessions we both tried to convince the committee as a whole that if they were serious about calling themselves "pro-choice," the diocese ought at least to provide a leaflet of resources for clergy and lay counselors to give to women that would include pregnancy care centers and social service agencies as well as abortion clinics, so that the concept of choice was real and not mere talk. We parted in camaraderie, but the leaflet never appeared.

Even when the committee was dismissed, I could not let go of the issue. I continually reexamined the arguments I had once used on behalf of legalized abortion, such as the claim that having unwanted children results in child abuse or that "compulsory pregnancy" (lack of access to abortion) contributes to economic inequality for women. Yet twenty years and millions of abortions later, the feminization of poverty is nearly complete and violence against children is a national disgrace. The myth closest to my heart held that women must be able to live without concern for unplanned pregnancy so that society would begin to regard us as human beings, not sex-objects and baby machines. Twenty years later, walk down to Times Square and then do a jump-shift to Wall Street. Not being "baby machines" means we are better sex machines and better cogs in the corporate machine. I found I could no longer define equality or freedom in these ways. Why did human existence have to revolve around bed sheets and ledger sheets? I hear again that woman whose voice I shut out for so long: "This is what you really think of us."

Meanwhile, things came full circle. I went to visit my daughter at college and she told me casually that she had been to a local pro-abortion march; she called it a "rally for reproductive rights." I didn't bore her with an analysis of the phrase "reproductive rights," and how I hear in it the kind of newspeak used in Nazi Germany, where the "Reich Committee for Children" was formed to kill physically and mentally handicapped children. All I said to her was this: You say you're a pacifist; so am I. But I hope you will think long and hard about whether a nation which sits back in silence while thousands of developing children are killed every day will ever be a nation that refuses to send its older children to kill and be killed in war. If we have no heart for the most helpless among us, how will we ever have any heart for anyone else?

I don't know what her answer will finally be. Perhaps she'll ask why the church doesn't provide assistance to women who find themselves pregnant and unready to face that responsibility alone. I ask that too. Yet I cannot help but remember that when it happened to me, there were Christians who were ready to shelter, feed, and nurture me. As I look around today, as growing numbers of neighborhoods and churches organize to provide help for women with unplanned or otherwise difficult pregnancies, I see that it is still possible to offer alternatives. With my embrace of the people who provided care for me in my first, unwanted pregnancy, something new and unexpected and deeply healing began in me. With my understanding that the illegality of abortion prevented me from casually undertaking an act of violence, my pacifism began to cohere.

SEVEN

Thank God for memory. Memory speaks when reason fails; memory consoles when the present is painful; memory disturbs when I am lulled into complacency. Memory reminds me how close I was to having an abortion in 1966, and how strong the temptation was in 1987. Memory also indicts me: without my conversion, without that book of essays picked up at random, without my trip to India, I might have been vaguely pro-choice or even indifferent all my life. Yet even more daunting to me are the continually appearing moral conundra with which I live.

Here are the twin girls born to Mary, a heroin-addicted mother with AIDS. They may not live long. As I gowned and gloved one evening during my year-long engagement as a hospital chaplain, preparing to change and feed these two little girls, I asked myself whether, if Mary had been diagnosed HIV-positive two weeks after she had found out she was pregnant rather than two weeks before she was due, I could have advised her against abortion. Or if she would have cared what I said, given her circumstances. Mary and her husband were my patients during their regular forays into the hospital for septicemia or overdose or whatever it was that time. They always asked my advice about their increasingly desperate conditions—as "regulars" in the social welfare network they were astute about the need of social workers to feel needed. Sometimes they even took the advice, a rare compliment.

Mary's babies had to be kept in the hospital until they were detoxed—that was the law. Mary was discharged a few days after their birth and went on a massive drug binge that nearly killed her. When she was readmitted half-dead a few weeks later, she managed to make the momentous decision to detox and enter a women's HIV program. I wish I could claim some responsibility for her getting straight, but I didn't see her from her discharge in late August after the twins were born until nearly Christmas, when she was off drugs and attending daily support group meetings. She scampered up and hugged me and eagerly began to tell me her story, her thin, pale face alive with hope and excitement for the first time since I had met her.

Meanwhile, as the twin girls passed their lonely days in neonatal intensive care, I went to see them whenever I was on duty. The neonatal unit was perpetually understaffed and the night nurses were always glad for another pair of hands. I felt I had some responsibility to these infants, one of whom weighed only two-and-a-half pounds at birth while her sister weighed four-and-a-half, so I went and changed them and gave them their bottles whenever I could. I had to put on sterile gloves to change one baby due to the possibility that she was HIV-positive, then put on another pair of gloves to feed her, then another pair of gloves to change her sister, and then yet another pair to feed her. I grew fond of the twins, who had funny little scrunched-up noses like their father, and I gave serious thought to trying to adopt them if Mary could be persuaded to surrender them for adoption. She did decide to surrender them (again, with no advice from me), but then I was counseled against trying to adopt. My husband and I were over forty and had two living children: we would be low on any list for adoption, even for these potentially critically ill twins. There were plenty of childless people who would want them.

One evening I went up to feed them and they were gone; their foster care placement had come through. Mary went to visit them every Saturday in foster care and would continue to do so until the adoption was complete; then she let go. She was in anguish over the adoption, but knew it was best for the girls. I told her about my child whom I gave up so many years before, and she could appreciate that I knew something of what she was going through. But it didn't take her grief away, just as no kindness or empathy ever diminished mine.

Another scene, another memory: a women's luncheon at my church, where I brought in a pro-life speaker. Perhaps she was a little rougher and a little more graphic than my mostly white, middle-class congregation was ready to hear. When she finished, a woman stood and denounced her, accusing both the speaker and me of having no compassion for all the babies with AIDS lying in hospital units without parents or hope. I was too appalled to tell her about Mary and her babies, or about my own child who had been adopted. The longer she screamed the clearer it was that the babies were not really at issue, for she knew nothing about the bureaucratic nightmare involved in arranging adoptions of ill, abandoned infants and seemed to have the naive notion that such children are there for the taking, like leftover bread in the local supermarket. But this woman was not advocating adoption; on the contrary, she thought such ill and unappealing infants should be done away with early on. She thought it was far better to abort a child who might have AIDS than to give the child the chance to live a little while.

She assumed she spoke for compassion, but what is compassion? What is the compassionate act? Yes, it is expensive to maintain these children. Yes, their lives are often short and lonely and painful, but so are many lives. The woman who was angry only knew these children through what she had read or perhaps seen on television: she had never held one, never fed one, never stood by while a tiny arm was being fitted with an IV. She may have meant well, but Mary's twins and the other struggling infants who inhabited the neonatal intensive care rooms were not people to her, they were abstractions, statistics, social problems. She could imagine them being better off if they had never existed because she had never seen or held one that did.

There is a movie called *On Giant's Shoulders* that used to be shown a lot on public television as a way of raising consciousness about the disabled. It isn't shown any more, and I suspect that might be because it makes a powerful statement about the value of "throw-away" human lives. *On Giant's Shoulders* tells the story of a boy born to a woman who had taken thalidomide: where he might have had arms and legs he had grotesquely truncated hands and feet. But in spite of his physical deformity and years in an orphanage, the boy, Terry, was intellectually and emotionally strong and articulate. (The young man actually portrays himself in the film.) When a working-class childless couple adopted him and gave him the family he longed for, Terry blossomed even more. His adoptive parents, meanwhile, had to fight to keep him. The whole story is a frontal assault on the idea that any human being, no matter how gloomy the prognosis, could have a life not worth living.

What about girls like Louisa, pregnant at twelve in the Catherine Booth Residence? Is it unfair to point out that whether she has her baby or has an abortion her life can go on, whereas there is no second chance for a life that has been ended? From what I remember of Louisa's rage, she was less angry at being pregnant than at a legal system that did not exact swift and strict punishment for criminals. For that is what a rapist, a child molester is: a criminal. We have some understanding of why such people act as they do, but as a society we know instinctively that such behavior is aberrant, anti-social, criminal. Leaving justice aside, is the victim better served by offering her a way to get rid of the evidence (abortion) or by assuring her protection, support, and the satisfaction of seeing her attacker convicted and imprisoned? What if our concern with abortion in cases of rape and incest is not "compassion" but an act of denial?

One of my closest friends in the seventies had an abortion and discussed it openly and proudly; she did it so as not to interrupt her professional advancement. Her husband similarly told his male friends how important this was—it was about women taking themselves seriously. Yet they were always careful not to talk about it in front of their five-year-old daughter. Within a year of the abortion their marriage had collapsed. When I was talked this over with my mother she said, "It's because of the abortion. They're acting out of guilt." I was indignant. Abortion was legal! Abortion was necessary! I sighed over how obtuse my mother was, even as my friend and her husband ventured into more and more sexual acting out. Eventually they settled down, not with one another, but not before causing some real damage to themselves and others, particularly their child. When I look back on it now, I think my mother was right. However good a face they were able to put on their choice, however much most of us who knew them supported them, their unwillingness to acknowledge the moral seriousness of what they had done eventually overpowered them. Freud called it the return of the repressed.

The girl in my high school who had an abortion in our senior year married the summer after our graduation. She married a man her father's age, one of her father's golfing buddies, and I remember feeling alarmed at her bridal shower because every other sentence was "Freddy this" or "Freddy that." I had been fairly close to this girl and abjectness was not her style. After I went to college, she wrote one or two brief letters. Two years later, she fled for her life: the man was violent. Eventually she moved in with her parents and found work in a women's clothing store, where I found her by accident years later on a shopping spree my parents bankrolled. "I don't know what went wrong," she told me when she recognized me. "It seems like nothing goes right for me anymore."

In India, at Shishu Bavan, Mother Teresa's home for children, I was shown a baby who had been rescued alive from a dumpster behind an abortion clinic, one of two late abortion survivors whom the missionaries had found and saved that year. A woman who didn't know me well sat in my living room and told me the story of how she aborted her fourth child when she was forty-five years old, and how the event came back to plague her with nightmares and uncontrollable crying. A student in my husband's class at the college where he teaches wasn't doing her work. She explained to him she was drinking heavily and felt compelled to hang around in cemeteries. She hadn't felt very good about herself since she'd had her abortion. A woman with a history of infertility described the two abortions she'd had in college and wondered if there was a connection. The pregnancy she achieved through in-vitro fertilization turned out at twenty weeks to be a Down's Syndrome baby, she told me, and she aborted that one too. She was very brave about her story, belligerent even, and dared me to challenge her. But her gray eyes were sad, and the emptiness of her life was another thing she didn't bother to deny.

These are "private" stories, from my own experience. There are "public" stories as well—public stories that make quiet statements about how we handle our conflicts around abortion. I find I was wrong to assume that most people are aware of even widely-reported stories about deaths from legal abortions, such as Dawn Ravenell, thirteen years old, who died from a legal abortion that her parents knew nothing about. Another adolescent story is just as disturbing: a young woman named Becky Bell died at the age of seventeen in an Indianapolis hospital. At the time, both her parents and pro-choice activists falsely asserted that she died from an illegal abortion and the story made national headlines. A follow-up report revealed, however, that the autopsy showed infection in her lungs, not the reproductive tract, and shortly before she died the doctor in charge told her parents he was not sure he could save the baby. Yet the fact that she died of a lung infection and that the baby may still have been alive when she was admitted to the hospital was never given the prominence of the first story and in some papers it was never discussed at all.[9]

Why ignore these unhappy stories? Many—though not all—women who have had abortions report being unhappy afterwards. Legalized abortion has failed to preserve women's lives as surely as it has failed to allowed them to be confident and calm about their choices. Yet a frank discussion of what has happened to women since *Roe v. Wade* is not taking place. If legalized abortion is an unmitigated benefit for women, why are its advocates so nervous about revealing its failures? Why is it so rare for pro-choice and pro-life advocates to join in taking action against unscrupulous and incompetent abortion providers? Why not publicly state that the death of Becky Bell had nothing to do with abortion?

It is not what we say, but what we do not say. Just as women are reluctant to discuss their abortion choice in public, they are equally reluctant to acknowledge the public fund of information about abortion that often gives short shrift to all our preconceptions, pro-life and pro-choice. In a recent review I wrote about a book on abortion, I quoted some of the most common statistics from abortion reporting, including the fact that half of all abortions are to terminate pregnancies that occurred from lack of birth control. This figure came from a widely-publicized Guttmacher Institute study, but I still received an irate letter from an abortion activist who insisted I had made it up. Even after I gave her chapter and verse for the reference, she was not satisfied; since I was the one who said it, it could not be true.

After the 1991 *Rust v. Sullivan* decision in the Supreme Court, the *New York Times* and *Dissent* both carried articles saying, "It is time to start telling the stories again." The stories they referred to were the stories of illegal abortions obtained prior to *Roe*. I have heard quite a few, and some of them are chilling indeed. But there is also a counter-narrative, made up of stories like the ones I have been telling, and I think it is time for these stories to obtain equal prominence and weight in the discourse of legalized abortion.

All of these people and their stories are very close to my heart. They are people I have carried in prayer and memory. They live among the threads of my life. Because of my love and involvement (even if only through prayer) with them, I know through them that there are no simple answers. Yet I am persuaded there must be a better way to deal with unplanned pregnancy, with disabled people, with rape and incest, than abortion.

A fruitful approach for Christians may be to talk about shame and healing. For all our culture's obsession with sex, Americans are still a people who understand that irresponsible sex and medically unnecessary abortions are shameful things. My son was stunned when letters appeared in *Spin* magazine criticizing the singer Sinead O'Connor for lamenting, on the one hand, the case of abused and starving children, and on the other admitting she had had an abortion in response to pressure from her record company. He was impressed to see how angry people were, people who might not otherwise be critical of abortion; its use as a tool of consumer capitalism became appallingly clear to him. The reluctance of abortion clinic operators to agree to follow-up studies on their clients again reflects their awareness that most women do not want their abortion choice widely known. The truth is, no matter how well one can rationalize abortion, it remains an unspeakable act.

Shame, after all, is not always a bad thing. Shame can prevent us from doing our worst. Some years ago I made an extended confession, and as I reviewed my life in preparation for it, I realized how many times I had desisted from some terrible act not by any strong moral sense but by my fear of being exposed and the subsequent shame. The defiant tone of some abortion narratives suggests a struggle with shame. I often wonder, too, whether the high rate of repeated abortions—currently between thirty and forty percent of all aborting women have had at least one abortion previously—means that some women feel compelled to repeat this traumatic act, perhaps in an effort to diminish its power over them.[10]

To know that one has done wrong, to acknowledge that wrongdoing, and to seek to make reparation where possible: these are the requirements of repentance, and important steps to wholeness and healing. My shame about the child I conceived, bore, and relinquished for adoption, and my shame about my failed marriage eventually compelled me to confession. It forced me to take stock of my life and find those things which I ought to change or restore.

What the church can do to assist this process of confession and healing is to become a community where shame and regret can be openly expressed, where healing can be offered. This will not be easy, for it will require in the first place a return to the vocabulary of sin and redemption, and a letting go of the language of therapy and politics with which we discuss so much human failing. One pastoral aspect of healing would be to allow the grief of childbearing losses, including abortion, a far more serious expression. When I was at seminary, one of my professors and his wife held a funeral for their premature, stillborn child. The year before, when Bill and I had lost our unexpected baby, the grieving and acknowledgment of loss released by reading the burial office in church was deeply healing.

When John Cardinal O'Connor suggested in 1992 that Roman Catholic dioceses maintain a "Tomb of the Unborn Child" to commemorate aborted babies, the outcry from pro-choice people was predictable. The cardinal may have had a political as well as a pastoral motive, but his pastoral sense was not far off the mark. In Japan the similar practice of *mizuko kuyo,* which began in the late sixties, is a way of memorializing aborted, miscarried, and stillborn children. A ceremony takes place in which the child is named and represented by a small statuette, usually of the Buddhist deity Jizo: "*Mizuko kuyo* is a tangible acknowledgment of what the religion holds is the unborn individual's reality...[which] gives women a vehicle for expressing pain over decisions that have often been forced on them."[11] While both Cardinal O'Connor's tombs and *mizuko kuyo* carry within them the potential to become maudlin, they nevertheless point to the human need for tangible manifestations of grief.

For the same reason I urge a wider use of the burial office, employing the lessons and prayers specific to children in cases of childbearing loss, including abortion. Some pro-lifers object to this use of the liturgy in cases of abortion, but I believe the potential for grief and guilt after abortion needs to be faced with prayer and sacrament. I do not think this represents a "tolerant" attitude toward abortion; indeed, using the burial office takes the reality of the unborn infant seriously and forces us to confront exactly what has happened: a child has died.

Today abortion has become a political act. That is how it is understood in public discourse, and why it is that even in church we rarely talk about sin when we talk about abortion. By *political* I mean that the very decision to have an abortion is a political decision. One is no longer making a moral decision, but aligning oneself politically, pro or con. Mothers of adolescent girls are well aware of how loaded with meanings abortion is, and how their daughters have come to see it as a rite of passage. Even in the early years after *Roe,* when decisions concerning abortion were still morally framed decisions, there was substantial seriousness about its meaning. Like war, abortion was not an act that a Christian could undertake lightly and then pray hard about afterwards.

Christianity has always taught its followers first to prefer the good. If an act or event is evil—that is, if it violates the good will God has for his creatures—it is to be avoided. If it is wrong, it is wrong. One important task of the church is to assist people in identifying and embracing what is good and shunning what is wrong. This discipline of identifying and avoiding what is unacceptable, no matter the cost or effort, is one way in which strength of character and purpose are developed. It used to be called formation. When the church loses a clear sense of what is wrong and therefore to be avoided, it can no longer guide its people in the formation of Christian character.

Now that abortion is a political act, it is also negotiable. Political acts, negotiable acts, however, are subject to power relationships. A moral act is not: when something is wrong, the person who refuses to do it has the ultimate advantage. And those who refuse to yield to immorality, like the righteous Gentiles who defied the Nazis to assist the Jews, demonstrate (often at the cost of their lives) what it means to assert that the wrong is not negotiable. But a political act, because it is negotiable, holds no one accountable; the "good" is whatever serves the moment. And as I have argued previously, the notion of the good in the development of abortion advocacy has not uniformly been to the advantage of women.

Those in favor of abortion under any circumstances argue that such advocacy has to do with justice. For Christians, however, "justice" does not mean forcing a social system to acquiesce to our needs; it has to do with righteousness, with "right being," and this is not a distributive concept. The so-called level playing field that Christian abortion advocates often propose as their rationale for legalized abortion cannot serve the call to righteousness because it proposes the freedom of the rich as the standard of justice for the many.

Sylvia Plath, the American poet who committed suicide in 1963, wrote a disturbing verse play entitled *Three Women: A Poem for Three Voices* that is constructed around internal monologues by three women in a maternity ward.[12] One of the women has had a miscarriage—or perhaps an abortion, for the language is ambiguous. She speaks of men as hating female fecundity, and as defining "the good" over and against what the women know in their bodies. Throughout the poem pregnancy is experienced with anxiety and thoughts of death; the efficient and sterile world of the hospital is in stark contrast to women's fruitfulness. Plath's poem is one indication among many of how the place of abortion in the common life of Americans as we approach the end of the twentieth century is at once so central and so troubling to who we are and how we locate ourselves in the national discourse. Increasingly, abortion must carry the burden of other, older, deeper fissures in the modern consciousness. How we finally come to resolve, or fail to resolve, the mind and heart of our nation in regard to abortion will be a marker of our ability to function not merely as a polity, but as a people with claims to honesty, civility, and charity.

I have tried to describe how I came to find myself, after all these years, after a life devoted to some kind of feminist certainty, opposed to abortion on demand. I tend not to call myself pro-life because I agree with Stanley Hauerwas that Christians don't believe in a "right to life," a truth to which the blood of martyrs for two millennia attests. At the same time, Christians are called to attend to the protection and the succor of the poor, the helpless, and the ill. I have seen so many on the streets of cities where I have walked or lived, from New York to Kampala to Calcutta, naked but for a shabby blanket, and it seems to me that the gospel compels me not only to prevent someone from stealing the beggar's blanket, but also to try to find food and shelter for her if I can. The developing child is, as far as I am concerned, much like the naked beggar and its fragile hold on life like the beggar's blanket. I am not of a confrontational temperament and I have grave disagreements with Operation: Rescue and with civil disobedience in general. Rather than demonstrate, therefore, I write, asking the forbearance of those who would steal the fetus's sole possession, life.

Conversation on the topic of abortion has become, in the long years since I entered the Catherine Booth Residence, exceedingly difficult. There is no longer coherent ground for discussion. Those with legalistic minds argue over the rights of the pregnant woman vis-a-vis the rights or lack thereof of the unborn child.

The scientifically inclined undertake abstract and bizarre researches into the subject of when the conceptus "becomes human," surely the modern equivalent of the scholastics' research to determine how many angels can dance on the head of a pin. Sentimental pro-lifers carry around photos of infants, some aborted and some alive, while sentimental pro-choicers display photos of women dead from illegal abortions. Paranoid pro-choicers see sinister plots lurking behind the anti-abortion movement—the end of abortion rights would mean the enslavement of women—while paranoid pro-lifers suspect abortion-rights advocates of seeking to impose a homosexual-communist Brave New World on all of us. The small but determined number of gays and liberals who oppose abortion are treated as if they didn't exist.

The language of the debate is revealing. When I first encountered feminist abortion rights activists in 1970 or so, the slogan they used was "Free abortion on demand" and they pointed proudly to socialist nations where this was available. In 1980, Ellen Willis, writing in *The Village Voice*, used the phrase "pro-abortion" to describe her support for *Roe*; in the mid-eighties, that term was gradually dropped and replaced by "pro-choice." The use of this word "pro-choice" is interesting because it suggests that what is actually being debated is the act of choice itself—an act that is personal, individual, and private—and not the act of abortion. This shift has been effective because it encourages people who are undecided about the morality of abortion to think about it in a way that validates their uncertainty. By repositioning the debate in the language of choice, abortion rights activists have drawn on the deep current of defiant American individualism: *You cannot legislate morality. I want to make up my own mind. Who do you think you are, to tell me what to do?*

At the same time, the term "anti-abortion" became "pro-life." Few people like being called "anti" anything, and the emphasis on "life" was meant to be a counterattack on the category of "rights" category. Therefore the unborn child's right to live was weighed against the woman's right to abort. Yet none of these locutions, in my view, get to the heart of what the current fight is about, which is whether abortion on demand should remain legally protected. Pro-legality and anti-legality might be more fruitful ways of describing the current concern of the respective positions. For there are certainly pro-legality people who are at heart anti-abortion, and they too have their contribution to make to the discussion.

Similarly, the language that speaks of what goes on in the event of pregnancy has altered. When I was on that diocesan committee studying abortion early in my struggle with the issue, I was struck by the insistence of the other women on the committee not to use the word "mother" to refer to a pregnant woman. This seemed to me to be a case of trying to avoid the obvious, but for those women it was a serious political statement. To be called "mother" was to imply relationship, a relationship that one had to be prepared to sever. Better to deny the relationship from the outset.

A few years ago, an op-ed piece in the *New York Times* was written by a pregnant woman who consistently referred to her unborn baby as "my fetus." The essay was not about abortion, and it struck me that her use of "fetus" for a third trimester baby was rather forced. I tried to remember being pregnant with Geoff in 1979 and felt certain people would have thought me daft if I had spoken of him as "my fetus" rather than "my baby." Of course fetus and baby are simply developmental terms common to mammals; a fetal pig is still a pig, a fetal cat is still a cat, and a baby calf is still bovine. Yet in the last ten years, fetus has become a catch-word that is meant to suggest that the developing infant is something less than human—a subspecies or alternate life form.

The verbal hedging is not all on the side of the pro-choice camp. I have already mentioned Stanley Hauerwas's rejoinder to Christians using the pro-life label. More disturbing, however, is the use of the term "innocent human life" by conservative Christians who want to keep the door open for war and capital punishment. This simply will not do. It is inconsistent to quote St. Paul's declaration on Sunday morning that all have sinned and fallen short of the glory of God, and on Sunday evening talk about "innocent human life," as if the unborn child is somehow exempt from human sinfulness while the killer on death row is undeserving of the mercy of God and the church.

The discussion, for me, must always return to God and the church. In answer to the central feminist question, "Who decides?" we need to reply carefully. The individual? The community? The church? In America we tend to assume that the individual decides, failing to notice that our emphasis on the individual has as great a potential for oppression as the communitarianism of many traditional societies. We forget that the ugly history of racism in America was buttressed by our obsessive individualism: I have the right not to serve the blacks or Indians or Chinese who come into my restaurant. While community-based ethics may overrule the individual in the name of the community, individualist ethics establishes a hierarchy of who counts. The unborn child does not count at all.

Christians are often reluctant to answer the question "Who decides?" by saying "The church." There have certainly been failures in the church's moral witness, from the Crusades to the theological rationalizations of slavery in America to the acquiescence of German Christians to Hitler. But there is also a history of courage and hope, and the witness of a long tradition of the church's repudiation of abortion cannot be cast aside without a second thought. What does this tradition say to us now? Perhaps that we have greater resources and more potential for welcoming the stranger than we ever had before, and it would be a sin not to share them with unexpectedly pregnant women and their children, living and not yet living. Perhaps because the Incarnation presents the entry of God into every stage of human life, Christians must be deeply skeptical of any teaching that would suggest that some people are irredeemably shut off from God. The faceless killer on death row comes again to mind, and with it, the more concrete image of John Paul II sitting with the man who had nearly killed him, offering forgiveness.

EIGHT

Uganda. Say it, and most people think of Idi Amin and the terror he brought. But Uganda means something very different to me, for I lived there from the summer of 1992 to the summer of 1994. My husband and I went to Africa to teach at Makerere University, in the city of Kampala. In retrospect, it seemed that many threads of our lives had been leading us to Uganda, but the immediate cause was a presentation at Bill's college by its president, who was on the board of the Rockefeller Foundation. She had been on a study tour of Africa to look over some of the projects the foundation supported. One of these was at Makerere University, and she spoke so movingly about what she saw there that Bill wondered if he had heard the voice of Jesus through her. He came to me and asked me what I would think about going to Uganda for a year to teach.

We had thought about trying to work abroad for some years. For both of us it was a kind of inchoate call, a sense that God had something in mind for us. We took to heart the old Quaker dictum, "Proceed as the way opens," and waited and prayed. In the fall of 1990, when Bill heard that talk, at least the timing was right: Shannon was doing well in college, and Geoff was young enough to take some time abroad without interrupting his education. As the winter and spring progressed, we continued to pray about it, and little by little the obstacles—including some we hadn't even known existed—disappeared. The last hurdle was funding, which was overcome when the Fulbright Foundation offered a fellowship to teach at Makerere. We got our vaccinations, contacted the International School in Kampala for Geoff, and packed our possessions for storage. I was ready to make a move of this sort, in part because I knew that Makerere wanted me to teach as well. A year of underemployment after leaving my lay position in a parish was making me restless, and the challenge of teaching Bible in an African university enthralled me.

When people ask me, "What do you miss about Africa?" I say, "The green." The morning we got off the plane at Entebbe was overcast and bleak, but by midday the sky had cleared and the equatorial sun dazzled us. The greens of the palms and banana trees, the grass and the flowers, had a luminous quality more intense and commanding than any vegetation I had ever seen. Other colors, like the lipstick red of the giant irises that grew everywhere, or the erotic purple of the conical pod that hangs at the end of a banana stem, only highlighted our encounter with the heart-stopping green of Uganda.

When people asked me during those two years we spent in Africa what I missed most about America, I often said, "Nothing!" My college roommate kept me apprised of the various weird and wild details of life in the U. S. via a steady stream of newspaper clippings. We missed bagels until Bill found a recipe for them and started making our own. For our second year we bought a computer, television, and VCR from people who were shipping out. There was a shop in town full of pirated videos from Dubai. It was sunny and seventy-five degrees nearly every day of the year. What was there to miss?

Nor did I miss out on the culture wars, in large part because many of the other Americans had dutifully carried them over to Africa. I had not been in-country two weeks when I was lectured at an American picnic about how I should support USAID's programs for massive condom distribution to combat AIDS. Since I was going to be connected to the Anglican Church of

Uganda, I was told, I ought to help convince the church to help with condom distribution. "If people don't listen to the church when it tells them to keep sex in the context of marriage," I asked the woman who told me all this, "what on earth makes you think they will listen when the church tells them to use condoms?"

That was easy for her to answer: because abstinence and monogamy are "unnatural" for Africans, and condoms will let them go ahead and have all the sex they want without fear of disease or pregnancy. This was a semiofficial representative of the U. S. government speaking; she must have assumed that because I was white and American I shared these racist assumptions. I started to explain to her why the church might not share her enthusiasm for condoms, but I was new in the country and didn't want to start off making enemies, so I changed the subject. It wasn't very long before I found out from a woman missionary that such sentiments were common in the "official" community.

For the most part, our closest friends in Africa turned out to be Africans. Ugandans seemed to me to be among the most hospitable people I had ever met. Once they had fed us—typically at sumptuous multicourse meals that lasted for hours and probably depleted the family food allowance for a month—they had practically adopted us. And once we were adopted, we began hearing the family stories. Among our university colleagues, we experienced a remarkable level of frankness and generosity. We tried to repay that generosity without looking like Lord and Lady Bountiful: we took their children out for ice cream when an ice cream parlor opened in Kampala, or we got people we knew in the States to send books we hoped would interest our new Ugandan friends.

Furthermore, because I was also teaching creative writing, I found things in stories and poems that told me more about my students and their homes and experiences than I might otherwise be privileged to see or hear. Particularly in the spring of 1994, as the massacres in neighboring Rwanda dominated our newspapers and conversations, my students' memories of the troubles in Uganda under Amin and Obote were released; their nightmares, their sorrows, and their fears returned like a flood. One young woman wrote of soldiers invading her boarding school and raping the girls; she escaped and wandered alone, on foot, cross-country for weeks until she reached her grandparents' home. An older male student wrote about his experiences in the rebel army that eventually established peace and a limited democracy in Uganda, while another student told of being kidnapped by a different rebel band that claimed that its female leader was Christ. For weeks the primary liquid she had to drink was her own urine. Brutality, casual violence, hunger, and despair had been the daily lot for many of my students during their childhoods. Reading their final manuscripts was one of the most emotionally gruelling experiences of my life.

It happened, as it always does, that the young women frequently wrote about sexual intimacy, and its difficulties, and by that route I began to find that abortion was a serious concern for educated Ugandan women. Most of the girls seemed to think it was a bad thing and ought to remain illegal in Uganda except when the mother's life was at risk, but they also understood very clearly that women may be driven to it from fear or desperation. It was uncanny to read their words: without any knowledge of my views on the subject, several young women wrote stories or essays that astonished me by their clear articulation of what could be called a pro-life feminist position. One young woman actually managed to get her essay published in a local newspaper, which made her—and me—ecstatic.

"Now people will know," Ann told me, "what drives girls to do this, the demands of men and the embarrassment of supposedly Christian parents." The essay concerned a young woman driven from home, abandoned by her boyfriend, eventually turning to a village midwife who induces an abortion, which the girl survives physically but broken in spirit. I did not know until much later that the person Ann was writing about was her own sister. Another young woman, Catherine, wrote a story about revenge in which a waitress in an expensive restaurant goes berserk and stabs a cabinet minister who is a patron there. It turns out she had had an affair with the minister, became pregnant, and then was abandoned. As she stabs him, she screams, "How do you like having a knife in your belly? That's what you forced me to do."

Sarah is a bright and talented Ugandan woman, a teaching assistant in the literature department at Makerere. One of her best stories concerns a secondary school student who is thrown out of her home because of her pregnancy. When I heard her read it, it gave me chills, sounding as it did very familiar. A few days later I asked her, "What's going on in this story?"

She laughed and assured me that it wasn't her own. For one thing, the mother in the story is the very image of the mean-spirited and pious woman who doesn't know she is forgiven and thus can't find it in herself to forgive anyone else. Sarah's mother died when she was a baby: she is one of many Ugandans for whom a life without one parent or indeed without any parents is normal. But while American children have to live with this because of abandonment or illegitimacy or divorce, Ugandans live with it because of war or AIDS or casual polygamy. However it comes about, many children and young adults in Uganda and America are growing up without a hint of what life might be like with both parents available, along with the emotional and financial security that such stability is often better able to provide.

Having reassured me about her own situation, Sarah began to explain to me the source of her story. The majority of secondary school education in Uganda is residential, which began under British colonialism as a copy of the British system. It has now become an economic necessity, in that primary and secondary school in Uganda is neither free nor universal, but a fee paying system. For families to afford to send children to school, adult members must work, often at two or three jobs. Younger children are cared for by housegirls or relatives, while the older ones spend most of their year at boarding school from the age of twelve to sixteen if they stop at O-levels, or until the age of eighteen or nineteen if they go on to A-levels. These ages assume that a child goes all the way through school from the age of five without interruption; some miss a year or more if the family cannot afford the fees. It is not uncommon for a person to get to O-levels at the age of twenty, and for girls, especially in the rural areas, the hopes of completing even O-levels are small.

Sarah attended a boarding school that is generally accepted as one of the best in the country. Her first anecdote was about a girl, the daughter of a doctor, who had gone home at midterm pregnant and come back at the beginning of the next term thin and frail and definitely not pregnant. The next was about a girl taken away in a coma with what proved to be a ruptured ectopic pregnancy. Sarah had started shyly, but once she began, the stories poured forth. Her first roommate at university who had, against all rules, a man in the room overnight. A girl from her village who appeared one day with a baby—no one knew where it came from. A very young, fat girl at the school where Sarah taught after her B. A. who gave birth in the bathroom because no one had guessed she was pregnant. Sarah did not have a note of condemnation in her voice. She felt genuinely and truly sorry for all these girls, but she was bitter about the men who were involved. "Their lives aren't ruined," she said. "They just go on doing what they have been doing. They don't have to leave school and they don't die."

The international aid organizations that provide sixty percent of Uganda's budget seem eager to bring in abortion. The Clinton administration's notorious cable to American embassies urging them to promote legalization of abortion in their host countries was no surprise: missionaries and other sources tell me this kind of pressure exists in East Africa already. For the past several years, the primary focus of USAID, the major American funding effort there, has been in agriculture. Near the end of my stay at Makerere, all the agriculture programs began closing down and the USAID hierarchy announced that the new funding focus will be "reproductive health." USAID's old focus on population control—once it was the largest funder in the world—may be coming back.[13]

My Ugandan friends are horrified when I tell them that this may mean a substantial push on aid-dependent countries to accept abortion in the future as a condition of their ongoing American assistance. With an American president whose first acts in office included a repeal of the ban on family planning funding to abortion providers, I do not imagine that Africans can expect forbearance in respect of their cultural preferences. Already the government-influenced Ugandan and Kenyan newspapers have reprinted articles from the foreign press suggesting that legalized abortion might be a good thing. Unfortunately, African nations are getting used to the demands of Western donors through the structural adjustment programs of the World Bank and the International Monetary Fund. Ugandans are none-too-politely urged to accept condoms as the correct response to AIDS and to abandon the government and church approved preference for "zero grazing," that is, abstinence. The power of the donor nations cannot be overemphasized, and the donor nations are very interested in disease and population control.

჻

Every year the International School in Kampala has a fair. The first year I was in Uganda I took my housekeeper's five children to the fair, and after I parked the car two women from the American community—one of whom was a friend—came up to me.

"Whose children are those?" asked one.

"My housekeeper's."

"Good heavens! I hope you've had a talk with her about birth control!" declared the other.

In fact, I had not had a talk with Madiina about birth control because she is a grown woman with considerable intelligence and self-respect, and I didn't think it was any of my business. We did wind up talking about birth control later that year, but not because I wanted to lecture her on not having any more children. What happened was that she began to bleed heavily and cramp and it turned out she was expelling the IUD she'd had for the past three years, thanks to the wife of the previous Fulbrighter, who was less squeamish than I. Now Madiina was without birth control and wanted to know what I thought she ought to do.

This was dangerous ground. I knew very well that many of the expatriate women thought it was their job to westernize their female domestics—getting them to use birth control and write wills and so on. These were all good things, certainly, if done with sensitivity. But I was determined not to impose my cultural preferences on my African friends and colleagues, and I was definitely not going to use my power as Madiina's employer to coerce her into behaving the way I wanted her to. I took Madiina to the dining room, poured us each a soda, and asked her what she wanted to do.

Her answer surprised me at the moment, but in retrospect, it shouldn't have. She told me she wanted to be done with men. She had had six children by three different men. The father of her three youngest, an older man she had been involved with for over ten years, had returned to his village to die the previous year (fortunately not of AIDS). The only man she still had sexual contact with was the father of her third child, a man from her home village whom she only saw when she went to visit her parents. The man had a wife, so there was no likelihood of a permanent relationship. Madiina was ready to chuck the whole thing—men, sex, the whole lot—and I think she wanted my permission to do it.

I was still trying to tread cautiously. Ugandan women, especially Baganda women like Madiina who are raised as Muslims, are socialized to a degree of passivity that Americans find maddening. In the aggressive traffic of East Africa, their passivity makes these women the most dangerous drivers. So I was still going to ask her to think about what she wanted.

"Do you love him?" I grew up on the music of the Supremes, so the question made sense to me. But Madiina just laughed. "No," she giggled, as if I'd asked if he had two heads.

"Do you enjoy it?"

She shrugged. "It's not like that, madam." I could never convince her not to call me madam. "They expect it. So we do it."

That was for me the definitive statement of what goes wrong between men and women. Our conversation went on, and we talked about how she could explain to this man that she had no interest in sex, and we talked about condoms, and we talked about what a deep problem sex is in general. She was amazed to hear that I had given a child away; none of her people would ever do such a thing. To think that one might have too many children—absurd! When I told her I was jealous of her large family, she was shocked. "We think the *bazungu* (whites) do not like children," she said shyly, "because they have so few."

. . . .

Sitting with a friend eating Chinese food in an excellent restaurant that overlooks Kampala, I described this conversation with my housekeeper. My friend Betty had just returned from the hospital bed of her husband's African assistant. The woman was dying of AIDS, and Betty was trying to convince her to write a will so that the family of the children's father could not claim the children and send them off to his village. The father also had AIDS; he had infected the woman. When he dies the children will have no one to defend them; they will have to rely on the benevolence of the family. Some families are more capable and willing than others to assist orphaned relatives, and the fact that there are comparatively few street children in Kampala (a mere handful, unlike Nairobi or Addis Ababa) says much for Ugandans' sense of family. But the number of orphans in some parts of the country is overwhelming the resources of elderly grandparents and one or two cousins who might have jobs.

Betty and I picked at our green beans in garlic sauce and wondered: are any of us—Americans or Africans—asking the right questions? Is the American yearning for pragmatic, achievable problem-solving leading us to ask the wrong questions? Betty has lived in East Africa for over ten years and has seen program after program to curb birth rates fall short. Africans, as Madiina taught me, actually like children. Two young women in my neighborhood once explained to me that when they marry, they will have small families—about four children each. I asked what they thought a large family was and they mentioned someone they knew who had seventeen children. That was too many. I didn't tell them that to the Euro-Americans who worry about population issues, four children is still at least two too many.

Betty and I have brooded over the fact that the single strongest indicator of family size is the level of the mother's education: the more years of school the mother has, the smaller her family is likely to be. Madiina's father did not educate his daughters past primary grade 7, and some of them not at all. This educational discrepancy is widely acknowledged, yet the nongovernmental organizations that fund family planning efforts spend an enormous amount of money on developing chemicals and videos and so on to convince women to have fewer children when the same money would be more effectively spent in the long run on paying to educate girls in poor countries. That is what I mean when I say that maybe our solutions aren't working because we are not asking the right questions.

In the abortion debate as well, we may be getting nowhere because we are addressing the wrong questions. The question at the bottom of most pro-choice statements is ultimately, Who decides? Who decides what women may choose as socially sanctioned (i.e., legal) behavior? The position of the American feminist movement is very much like Stanley Hauerwas's description of many current liberal theories of justice, which make all desires equal before the bar of justice.[14] That the desire may be potentially damaging to oneself and/or some other person is not in any way to serve as a bar to the desire, or the ability to act on it.

There is almost no way to address this question differently without recourse to what is commonly assumed to be religious language. To answer differently means to take the view that in our practices and our polity we have to have recourse to the meaning of "the good"—not only on behalf of the individual, but also on behalf of society as a whole. Even this is not necessarily a sure path to a case against abortion: some feminist theologians have argued that legal abortion is necessary to build a society in which abortion is unnecessary. That argument, of course, has within it the suspicion that abortion is ultimately an undesirable practice, and raises again the question of whether a desirable end can result from undesirable means. For most of history, the effort to construct a meaning for "the good" has included certain transcendent claims. Since the Enlightenment, however, transcendent claims have been displaced from public discourse and then discredited as unworthy of free people. Even in the church, to raise the question of transcendental claims and obligations beyond our own desires begins to look naive.

For Africans, transcendental claims may be more earthy and humane than we understand them in the West. Benezet Bujo, a Zairean Roman Catholic theologian, has written, "As for sexuality, this was valued in traditional Africa not as a source of pleasure, but for the sake of descendants. The ancestors laid upon every man the responsibility to provide survivors both for himself and for his clan." In Uganda children are not seen as the personal possession of the parents, to do with as they will, nor as individuals with neither a history nor a context for living, but rather as members of a web of life. Thus families, even if begrudgingly, take in the offspring of deceased relatives as a part of the larger obligation to the clan. And the clan obligation is not static or fixed in time. My children are my responsibility to my ancestors, my role in creating the future. Yet, Bujo argues, that is not all: to treat one's partner "simply as a source of children is to degrade them to the status of objects whose only worth is in their productivity. It is an example of the same achievement mentality which the African vehemently condemns in the industrial nations."[15]

A Danish aid worker I met in Kampala near the end of his tour was reflecting on his experiences in Africa. He had come to Uganda, like so many Europeans, to promote family planning and local health initiatives. He was leaving after four years, disturbed about what it was that he was doing. "We come here and tell these people that if they have fewer children, they will have more money and be happier," he told me. "Then I go back to Denmark on leave, and I look around me. I see lots of people with one or two children, if they have any, and plenty of money, and they are miserable. Are we really offering the Africans anything better than what they have? I don't think so anymore."

NINE

A man I knew a few years back married later in life and he and his wife decided not to waste any time having a family. She managed to get pregnant very quickly, but their happiness turned to sorrow when in the seventh month it was found that their child was severely malformed. The prognosis was as bad as could be imagined: the child might live a few hours after birth, if at all. Medical personnel and family members who knew the story urged them to abort. But something deep inside stubbornly told them not to. They took a bold step and announced in their church their unhappy situation, but they were not prepared for the strong show of love and support that the congregation gave them. Held up by the prayers and the casseroles of their fellow parishioners, they completed the pregnancy and their child lived long enough to be baptized. It was a terrible tragedy. But this couple was able to risk giving a brief moment of life to their damaged child because they were fortunate to belong to a church that did not expect silence of them or force them to go it alone.

In another church, a woman I knew found herself unexpectedly pregnant with a fifth child when she was over forty. She was near despair: "If I were to have a handicapped child it would not be fair to my other children," she told me. "What's fair?" I asked her. "Wouldn't it be fair to the other kids for them to learn how to love someone who is not, in the world's eyes, perfect?" It would be a gift to them, as it would be a gift to the church. People learn how much love they have in them when they are challenged to practice love. I urged her to talk to the people at her church, to build herself a support system, to let people help her through this. Oh, no, she said, I couldn't do that. Eventually, she submitted to amniocentesis, found that the baby was healthy, and carried out the pregnancy. But later, when the baby was older, she organized a support system for people in the parish who were having illnesses or babies or crises of whatever sort. What wasn't there for her, she's making available for others.

One of the most compelling rationales given for providing abortion even after the point of fetal viability is the possibility of a handicap or illness in the child. But I want to suggest that this is exactly the moment at which the church might most strongly want to resist the option of abortion. We are often told that it is wrong to bring a child into the world who will suffer. But is suffering the whole meaning of that child's life?

Handicapped people make the most extraordinary challenge to the church's complacency, and that doesn't merely have to do with building wheelchair access ramps. Handicapped people, particularly mentally handicapped people, force us to look squarely into our assumptions about what is the basis of our salvation. For far too many Christians, salvation is still something we earn. Whether we are conservatives who earn salvation by not drinking or smoking or by being pro-life, or liberals who earn salvation by running soup kitchens and writing letters to members of Congress opposing funding cuts to the arts, we have bought into the notion that we are saved by our works. Those whose "works" may be limited due to some disability embarrass those of us who for now find ourselves normally functional: what if I wound up in a wheelchair or without my sight? Then how would I prove how good I was, and how worthy of God's favor?

I have worshiped in two congregations where handicapped people were members of the congregation, and in both places I have been humbled by the witness of a handicapped parishioner.

In the church I served in England, I was assisting in the distribution of communion when I came upon Malcolm at the altar rail. Malcolm lived in a group home for people with multiple disabilities, and he and his friend Bernard were two of our most faithful members. That day Malcolm had his spastic hands twisted across his chest to signify that he was not going to receive communion. "Malcolm," I whispered, "what's wrong?" In unmistakable anguish he groaned, "I'm not good enough today." I have no idea what he thought he had done that the General Confession could not cover. But he did not receive communion that day, and he avoided the coffee hour (which he and Bernard normally revelled in). The following week he was his usual convivial self, but meanwhile he had led me to ponder over my own behavior regarding the eucharist, and whether I received the Body and Blood unthinkingly and thus unworthily—something that Malcolm, supposedly retarded, refused to do.

What these anecdotes have in common is their reflection of life in the church. For many American Protestants, the story I have told of the unexpectedly pregnant woman is the story of their relationship with the church: church is not the place where certain serious needs are met. The worship may be engaging, the music attractive, the Sunday school busy and well-organized, but when it comes to something like an unplanned pregnancy, the church has nothing to say or do for them. It is true that helping agencies like crisis pregnancy centers are more available than ever, but they tend to be para-church organizations, and mainline Protestant clergy steer clear of them. Women who find such agencies often find them through friends or on their own, not through the church, and even when such agencies are found they cannot always offer months of day-to-day assistance to families with handicapped children. All too often such families find themselves facing it alone.

The experience of the couple with the damaged unborn child is striking because it is so unusual. Americans are not uncaring or unwilling to assist their neighbors, but we have a tendency not to be forthcoming with our neighbors about our difficulties. While I am not endorsing the cult of chronic public confession that television talk-shows encourage, I do think that we have to be more willing to ask our fellow Christians for help when the going gets tough. I'm as guilty of such reticence as anyone else. Last winter I had to be hospitalized twice, and neither time did my husband ask our rector to visit me nor did I think to ask. After I was released from the hospital the second time, our rector chided me, saying, "How am I supposed to carry out my ministry if you don't tell me you're in the hospital?" The church as a whole might ask itself the same question: how are we to carry out our ministry of healing, reconciliation, and welcoming the stranger if we refuse to admit that we need healing, penance, and reconciliation, and that we know there is a stranger at the gate?

"It's *my* problem...I don't want to be a nuisance...Other people are worse off," we protest. No matter how we rationalize our reticence, our silence deprives the church of its opportunity to be the church. It is a courageous individual indeed who turns to his or her congregation in times of difficulty, and yet the extraordinary spectacle of small local congregations all over the country mobilizing to give care and comfort to a parishioner with AIDS should tell us just how undertapped is our potential for living as people of the gospel. In such circumstances churches are forced to deal with their anxieties about AIDS transmission, issues of sexuality and substance abuse, and the difficult confrontation with our own mortality. But if the formation of Christian character thrives as difficulties are taken seriously and overcome, then the congregation that has immunized itself against the suffering which is the daily human lot is a congregation which has placed a *Do not enter* sign on an important path to its own spiritual growth.

The church where Malcolm and Bernard worshiped was a church whose opportunity to be the church came as the result of a terrible tragedy. The vicar's five-year-old son was killed by a drunk driver. What might have been a private grief became a public one when the priest and his wife went to court to plead on behalf of the man who had killed their child and convinced the judge to place the man in treatment rather than in jail. The attention that this act brought the church eventually nearly doubled the size of the congregation, as ex-prisoners, interracial couples, Malcolm and Bernard—all people who had felt unwanted elsewhere—took the chance that in this place, perhaps, they would be accepted. There they were not only accepted, they were loved. A couple who was in the congregation throughout the entire period of transformation said, "Before, we didn't know the church could be like this. Now we can't imagine it any other way."

How might our congregational life be transformed? The New Testament has a number of ways of talking about what the church is supposed to be doing, but taken at its most basic, it tells us that Jesus took a practical, "hands-on" approach to people's problems. If the core of the Christian life is the imitation of Christ, then we are supposed to live like Jesus. This does not mean that Jesus is the standard by which we are to measure ourselves and invariably come up wanting; it means we are supposed to live like him in an immediate and ordinary way. For example, the disciples always wanted to send the crowds home to eat dinner but Jesus would not let them. "No," he said, "we do that here."[16] Feedings and healings are carried out by Jesus and his followers themselves, not by anyone else. Jesus' love was not mediated: it was direct, it was practical, and it was unconditional.

We in the church today cannot claim that the unconditional love found in the gospel witness has been extended to the unborn child or to the child's mother—who may be poor, or unmarried, or conflicted about childbearing. All the way from the evangelical colleges that James Dobson's report *Focus on the Family* found to be expelling pregnant female students, thus encouraging abortion, to affluent liberal parishes where clergy preach "freedom of choice" from the pulpit while not offering any alternative to abortion, American Christianity has all too often placed secular definitions of social morality above the call of Jesus to welcome and love the unwanted. This confusion has had consequences for the nation as a whole.

Watching on the nightly news the celebrations for January 22, the anniversary of *Roe v. Wade,* my husband noted that all the featured leaders of the pro-choice group were Hollywood celebrities. He reminded me that during the days of the civil rights movement, we drew strength from a leadership in which major figures of Christianity and Judaism were heavily represented. No matter how alienated we were from religion at the time, we knew that the presence of men like Martin Luther King, Jr., Paul Moore, and the Berrigan brothers displayed that passion for righteousness for which the church, at its best, stands. Today we have movie stars and other celebrities defining ethical issues for our children.

But history demands harsher questions. Can we say in all honesty that we are a better and happier and more productive people than we were when I was a teenager just out of high school and living in a home for unwed mothers? If we are the pragmatists that the rest of the world admires, can we say that twenty or more years of legalized abortion has improved our nation in any way? Does the poverty of the increasing numbers of female-headed households tell us anything about our failure to take the needs of women and children seriously? As far as the churches go, conservative churches have kept to a secular and conservative political view, while so-called mainstream churches have followed the trend of liberal politics. Only in a few out-of-the-way places have Christians—Mennonites, for example, and Roman Catholics in the Catholic Worker tradition—been willing to turn to the gospel, no matter how difficult that is, and ask what Jesus would do, or what Paul might say.

Within the Christian tradition we have some distinct and concrete practices that ought to enable us to serve our sisters and brothers when they are experiencing serious trials in their lives. The word "serve" says much: a parish-based servanthood ministry to women—and men—facing crisis pregnancies is desperately needed. The experience of AIDS ministry is a useful model. Such ministry has to be practical, not confrontational, providing medical care, daily encouragement, job training, and hope. We must not submit to the counsels of despair that tell us, "Women will always have abortions." We have another, a greater, counsel to offer, if only we will. For he came to give us life, and to give it abundantly.

People in pregnancy assistance ministries do have to face some unhappy truths regarding adoption. I began writing this book in large part because at one pro-life conference I said some rather uncharitable things about the glibness with which some of the other participants spoke about adoption. Since then, I have seen with horror small children wrenched from the arms of adoptive parents and returned by the courts to birthparents who changed their minds years later. I understand all too well the sense of loss and pain that someone may feel after surrendering a child, but once that child is placed in a new family, the birthparents must let go. Giving up a child for adoption is agonizing, as I hope my narrative conveys, and it is the duty of those who assist pregnant women planning to give their child for adoption to help them prepare for and then live with the pain of the loss. We must make it clear that no pain or trauma we may experience is anything like the pain and trauma of a child of three or four torn from the only parents she or he knows, and delivered into the hands of strangers. In the depths of despair it is hard to find consolation, but if the church is forming Christians as it ought to, then it will offer healing and affirmation to women who have made the decision to continue an unlooked-for pregnancy. After either abortions or adoptions, women don't live happily ever after.

One way to appreciate what the church uniquely has to offer is to remember our baptism. I was nearly done with seminary when I was placed in a situation in which I learned something about baptism that no book or lecture could ever have taught me. The hospital where I spent a year as a chaplain had a chaplain on duty twenty-four hours a day. Many of my shifts were Friday and Saturday nights, when the full-time chaplains did not particularly want to work. At first I mostly read prayers at the time of death and prayed with those scheduled for surgery. Then as the emergency room staff got to know me, I was called for beaten women, people with gunshot wounds, confused street people. A little girl on a gurney with two broken arms, the handiwork of her mother's boyfriend, made me angry in retrospect, but I had long since ceased to be shocked or surprised by anything. I called police and social workers; I talked to the child and her sister who would not leave her side; I reassured them that the bad man who had hurt them would be kept away from them. I always felt as though I could "do" something.

But the day came when my "doing something" had to die in the face of what God was doing. I was at dinner when my beeper went off and called me to the neonatal intensive care unit. A nurse I knew stopped me at the door and warned me that I was about to see a severely deformed baby. The baby had been found to be hydroencephalic (water on the brain) and microencephalic (what brain there was was grossly underdeveloped). The hydroencephaly was so severe that she could not be delivered normally. Her mother had consented to having a probe brought into her womb that would drain the water off the baby's brain so that the baby could be delivered vaginally. But the probe also collapsed the baby's skull. After birth, she was found to have other congenital defects. Somehow she was still alive, and her parents wanted her baptized.

I had never baptized anyone before. I knew that any baptized Christian can perform a valid baptism, but I felt unequal to this. However, in the eight-hundred-bed teaching hospital, I was the only chaplain. I think it was St. Teresa of Avlia who said, Christ has no hands in the world but yours. That night, the hands were mine.

I gloved and gowned and carried my prayer book into the neonatal intensive care unit. Stephanie lay in a clear plastic crib, her head swathed in gauze. Her eyes were wide and fixed. Like any newborn, she was swaddled, but somehow for this child it was particularly pathetic. The nurse asked me if I thought she was still alive.

It was not the first time that a member of the medical staff had turned to me and asked if I thought someone was dead, or if the machines could be turned off. At first I had been perplexed, but gradually I realized that many members of the hospital staff—for all their scientific training—had a strong intuitive sense that death was not just a matter of flat lines on a monitor. Death was a spiritual issue as much as a medical one, and they turned to me because I was the staff member (for better or worse) whose job it was to attend to spiritual matters.

In reply to the nurse, I bent down and blew gently on Stephanie's eyes. She blinked. "She's alive," I said. It was a little trick I had learned from the Missionaries of Charity in India. Blowing on the eyes of the sick and dying was their low-tech way of determining who was alive.

I asked for a basin of water and was given a nursing bottle of sterile water. I asked a nurse to serve as my lectern and hold the prayer book. I broke the seal on the nurser, removed the lid, and blessed the water. We thank you, Father, for the water of baptism....

My gloves were slippery. I poured the water awkwardly into my hand. *I baptize you in the name of the Father and of the Son....*

As the water touched her head, Stephanie shuddered. Her small dark eyes met mine, and suddenly I saw eternity open. For a second that seemed to last forever, I saw this wounded child as God must have seen her: beautiful and whole. Her life became to me infinitely precious. There was nothing in my life that I had ever done that mattered so much as what I was doing right then, and there was no child more beloved of God than this child.

...and of the Holy Spirit.

I made the sign of the cross on her forehead. Her father, who had slipped in beside me, was shaking with unshed grief. I turned to him. Still carrying the nurser of sterile water, I went out into the corridor to pray with him. An hour later, Stephanie died.

For a long time afterward, I saw in this event a justification for infant baptism. I felt that Stephanie's baptism was a gift to her and her parents—her incorporation into the Body of Christ and her parents' assurance of their baby's eternal life. I saw it as a healing event for all of them. But later I began to appreciate the ways in which it was a healing event for me, too. On the immediate level I learned that I was not called upon to "fix" anything: I was simply God's available instrument. That awareness freed me from the idea that I had to be wise or influential. I could let God do the work.

Later still, my spirit traveled back to the moment when God allowed me to glimpse Stephanie through his eyes. It occurred to me that God sees me as he sees the Stephanies of this world—beautiful and whole. Yes, he knows my faults, but the water of baptism clothes us in the robe of Jesus' righteousness. Like the parent who can see the sweet child in the less-than-pleasant adolescent, God loves to see us as he meant us to be, and as we will be when we are with him at last. This is the God who saw in the heart of a poor and obscure girl the strength and faith that would be necessary for the mother of the Redeemer, the God who rejoiced in the brash and impetuous personality of a fisherman and made him the leader of the movement which came into existence in response to that Redeemer. It is the God who loved so completely that he took it upon himself to join us funny and foolish creatures made in his image, so that all creation could be made new. Those of us who live in the hope of his coming again have the wonderful opportunity to assure our friends and families that there is no trouble into which God's grace cannot enter, and there is no event that God's love cannot ultimately turn to the good. Baptism steadies us as we walk with God in reconciliation and rejoicing, and baptism keeps us on that track, even when it seems that everything else is falling down around our ears. My whole life is evidence of that.

I have no gripping conclusion. I have only the sum of my stories, which I hope are entered into the greater story, the story of God's work in the world. I truly believe that God's story requires that we examine our stories, and ask ourselves questions that may be more daunting than those we have asked before. Will our answer be the despairing one of so many, who say there is too much illness, too many people, and too many burdens for the rest of humanity to be asked to bear? Are these the right questions? And if not, what are the essential questions, the ones that every generation needs to learn to ask again? Who is my neighbor? Who do you say that I am? Friends, what shall we do? I hope we will answer as Christ himself did: heal the sick, welcome the stranger, trust in God and let his perfect love cast out our fears. Work and pray: it is what we are called to do and what we must continue to do until his coming again.

EPILOGUE

I completed the first draft of this book while we were living in Uganda. Two weeks after I finished it, I went to the United States Information Service office in Kampala, Uganda to pick up our twice-weekly mail delivery, which included a 5 x 7 brown envelope with an institutional address I didn't recognize. As I walked to the car I tore the envelope open (I typically look first at the things I can't identify) and discovered inside a brief note from a social worker. Her letter was paperclipped to another envelope, a plain one, and in that was a five-page handwritten letter from my first son, who had decided to research his adoption.

Several years previously I had placed my full name and address in my son's adoption file. For a long time I heard nothing. Somehow I thought results—the appearance at the door of a handsome, eager young man—were immanent, but nothing happened. I wondered if his parents had told him. Maybe he wasn't interested. Sometimes I allowed myself to admit my worst fear, that perhaps he wasn't alive. As I had decided not to search for him, I feared I would never know anything more about him this side of eternity. Still he had lived on for me in memory, a sleepy tiny boy who looked a lot like his father.

And then his letter, completely unexpected, arrived. As shock, joy, fear pulsed through me, I did the best I could to get to the home of a missionary couple I knew. They prayed with me and made me tea and held my hand as I read that extraordinary letter. Later when I had calmed down, I gratefully took my leave. As I cooked dinner I gave my husband and son the letter to read. I think they were as stunned as I was.

He told me his name was David. From then on he and I began to correspond, at first with a kind of extravagance and urgency. We were shocked and amused, throughout the early correspondence, to find how similar we were. He is a high school English teacher, passionate about education, interested in completing a doctorate, in love with books. He grew up in a small town in the midwest and recalls a happy childhood of reading early and playing intensely with matchbox cars. He is devoted to his parents, considers his father his closest friend, spoils his niece and nephew. Like me, he's nervous about heights and considers rollercoasters the amusement from hell. And he's an Episcopalian, though he is a "cradle" while I am a convert.

When after a year or so I explained to him my views about abortion, he replied that it had always struck him that abortion advocacy seemed an anomaly in liberal politics. If the premises of twentieth-century liberalism are based on the protection of the defenseless and social intervention to advance the care of those unable to care for themselves, then abortion simply does not fit. He and I have debated this problem in many letters and in person, and his insight has been helpful to me in clarifying some of what I say in this book.

He visited us at home last year during Holy Week. The day he was due to arrive, I was skittish, and plumped cushions and wiped down counters and jumped every time the dog barked. Then at about five-thirty Bill, Geoff, and David all arrived at the same time and walked through the door. Bill and I had worried that Geoff would feel pushed aside. Whether he intuited this or whether he was simply eager to befriend us, David quickly established a bond with Geoff—so much so that the second night he was here, the two of them ganged up and forced me to watch "Beavis and Butthead" with them. David and I had a packed day of museum-going in Manhattan, and David and Bill worked over the cutting edge of literary criticism. Having him around was like having an old friend, with whom one had been out of touch, come back into one's life.

There is one thing David definitely does not get from me: he's an avid runner and athletic coach. I consider my thrice-weekly workout penance. When he visited I took him to our gym, which is a high-tech set up with a track, pool, and weight training space. From where I labored on the exercise bike I could see him running on the track above. He had an easy grace as he ran, and for the first time I understood the runner in the movie *Chariots of Fire* who said, "When I run, I feel God's pleasure." David ran like someone who was feeling God's pleasure, and it was a pleasure to watch him.

Where this new friendship will go next I cannot say. I try to back off from encouraging David too strongly to study for his doctorate, although I think he'd be brilliant, and I don't have much counsel for the one great lack he feels in his life: he would like to be married and starting a family. On the other hand, as he describes his high school teaching, I feel certain he is making an enormous difference to his students.

I do not say that being in contact with him has brought the events I have described in this book to a close. A new chapter has opened, which has helped me examine the past in ways I never imagined possible. Healing continues. The missionaries I prayed with the day David's letter arrived gave me a Bible verse, a promise of God's faithfulness in the midst of our loss: *I will restore to you the years the locust has eaten. (Joel 2:25)*

NOTES

1. Frederica Mathewes-Green originated this analogy. See her interesting account of its use by the pro-choice movement in *Real Choices* (Sisters, Oregon: Multnomah Books, 1994), pp. 18-19.
2. Report of the committee "The Family in Contemporary Society," 2.148, *The Lambeth Conference 1958* (London: SPCK and Greenwich, Conn.: Seabury Press, 1958).
3. Reported in *The New York Times* (January 18, 1967), p. 14.
4. James Tunstead Burtchaell, C.S.C., *Rachel Weeping: The Case Against Abortion* (San Francisco: Harper and Row, 1982), p. 230. Also Nanette J. Davis in *From Crime to Choice: The Transformation of Abortion in America* (Westport, Conn.: Greenwood Press, 1985).
5. Passed at the 69th General Convention and reaffirmed by the House of Bishops at the 70th General Convention.
6. Feminists for Life of America, *Man's Inhumanity to Woman Makes Countless Infants Die* (Washington, D.C.: Feminists for Life of America). See also James Mohr, *Abortion in America: The Origins and Evolution of National Policy* (New York: Oxford University Press).
7. In the 1980s one study suggested that nearly ten thousand abortions were performed per day in the Soviet Union, with an average of three to five abortions per woman. See "Family Planning and

Induced Abortion in the USSR" by Andrej A. Popov in *Studies in Family Planning* 22:6 (1991). An American woman doctor met women in the Georgian Republic who relied on abortion for birth control; one woman had had ten abortions. See Libby Antarsh, "Six Children and Ten Abortions in Fifteen Years," *The New York Times* (December 12, 1992), op-ed page.

8. Burtchaell's *Rachel Weeping* does a stark analysis of the similarities between Nazi and pro-abortion rhetoric, in which he takes careful note of the resistance to such a comparison. See also Burtchaell, pp. 244, 223, 61-65.

9. Mathewes-Green, *Real Choices*, pp. 101-104. *New York Times* reporter Linda Greenhouse and columnist Anna Quindlen both reported that Becky Bell had died of complications from an illegal abortion. When investigative reporting by Sue Halpern of the *Louisville Courier-Journal* and Joe Frolick of the *Cleveland Plain Dealer* showed that her death was not abortion-related, the *Times* did not provide a correction or a follow-up.

10. Findings from the Alan Guttmacher Institute in 1989 showed that over forty percent of women who have had one abortion return for one or more repeats (*New York Times*, May 8, 1989); a more recent study suggests these numbers are now declining. But as Tietze, Forrest, and Henshaw reported in the *International Handbook of Abortion* (ed. Paul Sachdev [Westport, Conn.: Greenwood Press, 1988]), during the first ten years after *Roe* the number of women who had had at least one abortion, and the number of repeat abortions, increased at nearly the same rate. As the number of women who have had at least one abortion increases, there is a larger pool of women at risk for repeat abortions.

11. Peter Steinfels, "Beliefs," *The New York Times* (August 14, 1992), p. 9.

12. Sylvia Plath, *Winter Trees* (New York: Harper & Row, 1972), pp. 45-63.

13. Betsy Hartman, *Reproductive Rights and Wrongs* (New York: Harper & Row, 1987), p. 104. Hartman's book, written from a pro-choice stance, is a compelling condemnation of population control practices in the Third World. My own experience abroad convinces me that her analysis of the situation is valid.

14. Professor Hauerwas made this remark "off the cuff" in his Trinity Institute Lectures of 1989. More formally put, "The problem with most contemporary political philosophies is not that they are individualistic, but that in the absence of any account of the good, individuals are led to believe that all their needs are legitimate." See his chapter, "Why Justice is a Bad Idea for Christians" in *After Christendom* (Nashville: Abingdon Press, 1991).

15. Benezet Bujo, *African Theology in Its Social Context* (Nairobi: St. Paul Publications, 1992), pp. 69, 120.

16. I am indebted to the Revd. Linda Strohmier for this insight.

Cowley Publications is a ministry of the Society of St. John the Evangelist, a religious community for men in the Episcopal Church. Emerging from the Society's tradition of prayer, theological reflection, and diversity of mission, the press is centered in the rich heritage of the Anglican Communion.

Cowley Publications seeks to provide books, audio cassettes, and other resources for the ongoing theological exploration and spiritual development of the Episcopal Church and others in the body of Christ. To this end, it is dedicated to developing a new generation of theological writers, encouraging them to produce timely, creative, and stimulating publications of excellence, and making these publications available widely, reaching both clergy and lay persons.